Animalium

For James – K.S.
For Edwin, lover of facts – J.B.

BIG PICTURE PRESS

First edition published in the UK and Australia in 2014 by Big Picture Press,
This edition published in the UK in 2017 by Big Picture Press,
an imprint of Bonnier Books UK,
The Plaza, 535 King's Road, London, SW10 0SZ
www.templarco.co.uk/big-picture-press
www.bonnierbooks.co.uk

5 7 9 10 8 6 4

ISBN 978-1-78741-164-7 (This edition)
ISBN 978-1-78370-129-2 (Collector's edition)

Printed in China

The book was typeset in Gill Sans and Mrs Green
The illustrations were created with pen and ink and coloured digitally

Written by Jenny Broom
Designed by Mike Jolley

With thanks to Valerie Davies and Katie Cunningham

FSC
www.fsc.org
MIX
Paper from
responsible sources
FSC® C010256

Animalium

Illustrated by KATIE SCOTT

Written by JENNY BROOM

BPP

Preface

Planet Earth is the only one we know about so far that has life on it, and where living things have evolved to become both numerous and diverse. We share our planet with about 2 million other species of living things – and these are just the ones we know and have given names to.

This diversity of life is called biodiversity, and although it might seem far away and not part of our daily lives, biodiversity is what keeps the Earth a good place for us to live. Because we, humankind, are another species of animal, like a fly or a jellyfish or a giraffe, we too are part of biodiversity, and we share our planet with each and every species.

The variety of animals on Earth is amazing. Most are insects, and very small, and some animals you just couldn't make up! But while they might look strange to us, they too have a role in making the Earth fit to live in. The diversity of life on Earth is what sustains us – without it there would be none of the food we eat, nor the air we breathe, but perhaps even more importantly, without it there would be no imagination.

It is only from things we know that we can begin to imagine things that are different and to tell stories. Each different creature is a starting point. These pictures in *Animalium* are of real things, and each sparks a new thought. Each too has a home on Earth, and I hope we can imagine a future where humankind can share this planet better with all of this wondrous diversity. The Earth, ultimately, is home to each and every one of us…

Dr Sandra Knapp
Natural History Museum, London

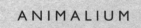
Welcome to Animalium

This museum is unlike any you've visited before. Open twenty-four hours a day, seven days a week, its collection boasts an unrivalled catalogue of the world's finest and most extraordinary creatures, with each exhibit in immaculate condition and presented in fantastic detail.

Wander through the pages of the museum to tour its galleries and see the story of life on Earth unfold. Every chapter takes you to a different part of the museum which displays a particular class of animal, such as reptiles, birds or mammals. The species are arranged in evolutionary order to show how the animal kingdom has developed over time. See for yourself how the tree of life evolved from the simple sea sponge into the wild and diverse array of animals to be found on Earth today.

Pause to inspect each exhibit carefully. Some rooms showcase a group of related animals; look for characteristic similarities and read the text to find out more about why these animals are comparable. Others give you the chance to enter the museum's dissection laboratories, where the animals' skeletons and internal organs can be studied.

Passing through the museum's halls, discover terrariums and explore the habitats encased there, filled with life in all its forms. See how different climates support different ecosystems, and learn how species have evolved over millions of years to become perfectly adapted to their surroundings.

This is the only museum to house animals ancient and modern, enormous and tiny, vicious and vulnerable between two covers, so enter *Animalium* and see the animal kingdom in all its glory.

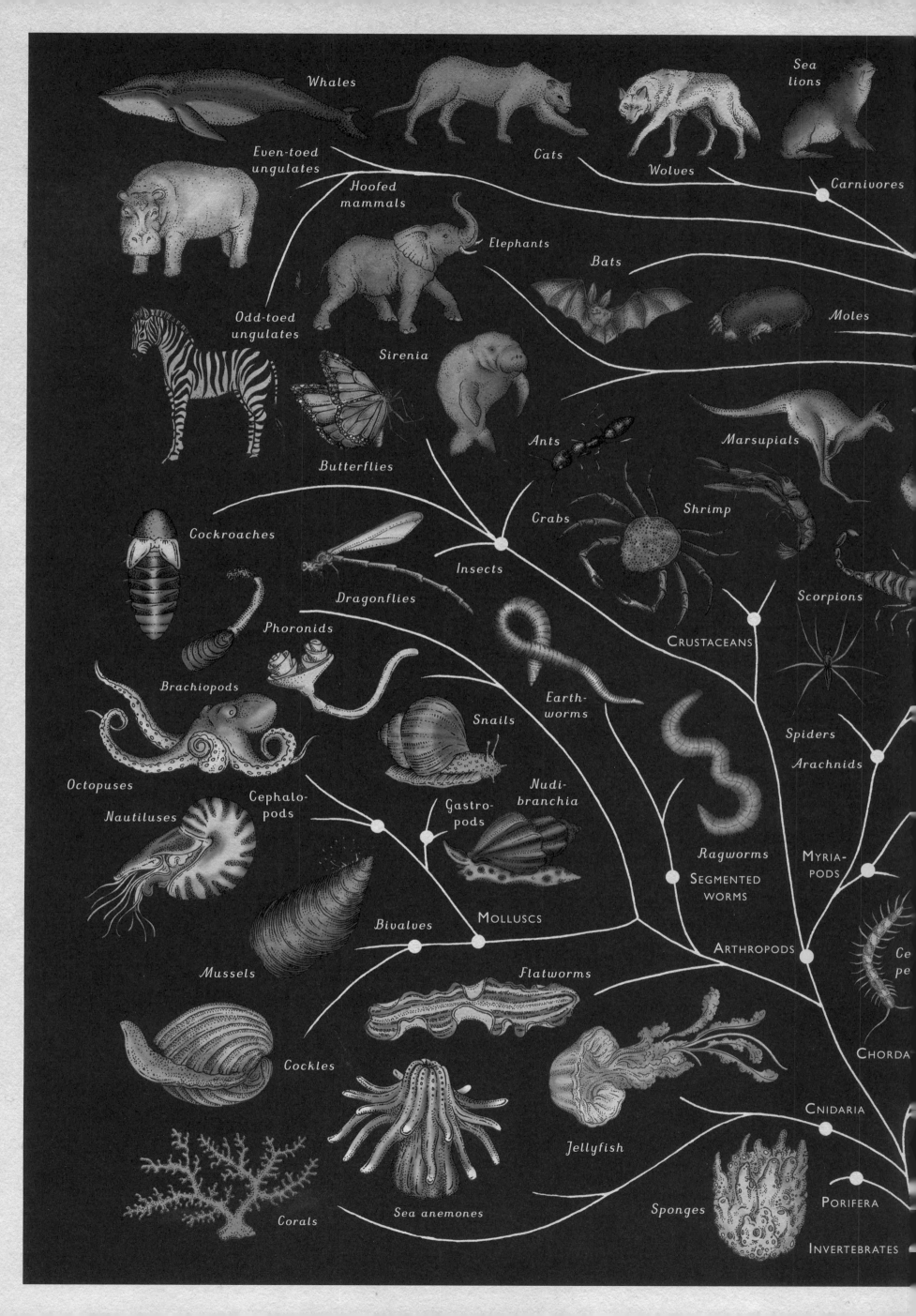

Whales

Even-toed ungulates

Hoofed mammals

Cats

Wolves

Sea lions

Carnivores

Elephants

Bats

Moles

Odd-toed ungulates

Sirenia

Marsupials

Butterflies

Ants

Shrimp

Cockroaches

Crabs

Scorpions

Insects

Dragonflies

CRUSTACEANS

Phoronids

Brachiopods

Earthworms

Snails

Spiders

Octopuses

Nudibranchia

Arachnids

Nautiluses

Cephalopods

Gastropods

Ragworms

MYRIAPODS

SEGMENTED WORMS

Bivalves

MOLLUSCS

ARTHROPODS

Mussels

Flatworms

Ce
pe

Cockles

CHORDA

CNIDARIA

Jellyfish

Corals

Sea anemones

Sponges

PORIFERA

INVERTEBRATES

Humans

Apes

Lemurs

Primates

Monkeys

Kiwis
and ratites

Penguins

Parrots and
cockatoos

Rodents

BIRDS

Crocodiles
and alligators

Birds of
prey

Rabbits

Placentals

Lizards

Snakes

Storks, ibises,
and herons

gg-laying
notremes

Reptiles

Mammals

Turtles and
tortoises

Amphibians

Urodela

Lungfish

Frogs
and toads

Newts
and salamanders

Mites

Lobe-finned
fish

Salmon and
trout

Millipedes

Cartilaginous
fish

Ray-finned
fish

Carp and
goldfish

Sharks

Jawless fish

Lampreys

Skates and rays

ERTEBRATES

Sea squirts

Larvaceans

Lancelets

TUNICATES

CHINODERMS

Sea urchins

Brittle stars

Starfish

Crinoids

Sea cucumbers

The Tree
Animal Life

Tree of Life

The tree of life is a lot like a family tree. It encompasses all of the animals on the planet and shows how each genus is related. It visualises, on a very basic level, how organisms which appear to be very different have, in fact, evolved from one another over millions of years.

Charles Darwin illustrated the tree of life in *On the Origin of Species* in 1859. In this book, he concluded that all life on Earth was related and descended from a common ancestor. Since that time, we've broadened our understanding of genetics, biochemistry and DNA, and those scientific endeavours indicate that a lot of Charles Darwin's ideas were probably right. Modern science indicates that eukaryotes – organisms whose cells have a clearly defined nucleus – like animals, plants, algae and fungi, do appear to share a common ancestor.

The earliest – and simplest – organism is located at the base of the tree of life. As species have evolved, adapting to survive in particular habitats, they are shown on the diagram to branch away from the original stem. Hence, the further a species is located from this base point, the more evolutionary modifications it has undergone.

These adaptations happen gradually over many generations. Characteristics that give an animal an advantage in its chosen environment increase its chances of surviving and reproducing, and thus of passing its genes on to its offspring. This theory, known as natural selection, lets us understand how the millions of species on Earth today have come into being over time.

ANIMALIUM

Gallery 1

Invertebrates

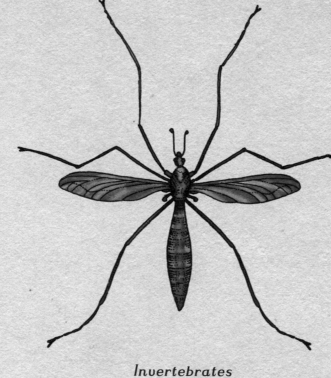

Invertebrates

Porifera

Cephalopods

Cnidaria

Flying Insects

Habitat: Coastal Waters

Invertebrates

Invertebrates are grouped together not because they have significantly similar features, but because they all lack a very important one: a jointed spine. The term *vertebrate* comes from the Latin word *vertebratus*, for 'joint'. *Invertebrate* therefore means 'without a jointed back'.

The term *invertebrate* refers to animals from across several evolutionary branches that, in some cases, are very distantly related. Consequently, invertebrates vary wildly, from the simple sponge to the complex and intelligent octopus.

Most species of invertebrate evolved around 540 million years ago, making them Earth's earliest animals. And whilst vertebrates – those species that evolved to have a jointed spine – often outdo their spineless cousins in size and intelligence, invertebrates come out ahead in numbers, making up around 97 per cent of the animal kingdom. Their successful evolution story means that they can be found almost everywhere on Earth: in water, in the air, on land and even underground.

Invertebrates can be divided into related groups, which include sponges, Cnidaria (such as jellyfish), flatworms, segmented worms, molluscs (including cockles and mussels as well as octopuses and squid), arthropods (including insects, arachnids and crustaceans) and echinoderms (such as starfish).

Porifera

Porifera, or sponges, are thought to be the first phylum, or overarching category of animal, to evolve from the earliest life-forms, single-celled creatures called protozoa. Fossils found in southern Australia suggest that sponges were living in the waters there up to 665 million years ago. The evolution of the multicellular sponge all those millions of years ago was one of the most significant developments in natural history.

Living exclusively underwater, sponges can be found in all habitats, from tropical seas to icy waters. With no nervous system or organs, sponges are incapable of thought or movement, and it would be easy to mistake them for plants. However, sponges are in fact animals that live underwater, feed on bacteria and sense and react to their environments.

Although they come in many shapes, colours and sizes, sponges all have structures based around a hollow central cavity (a bit like a chimney) surrounded by several small holes. This design allows water to flow through the sponge's central channel, nourishing it with food and oxygen and carrying away carbon dioxide. Some contain chemicals with medicinal properties, which make them useful to humankind.

Key to plate

1: **Cross-section of bath sponge**
Spongia officinalis
Length: 35 centimetres
This sponge is found predominantly in Greek waters at depths of up to 40 metres. Its shape is generally round.

2: **Calcareous sponge**
Leucosolenia botryoides
Length: 1.2 centimetres
This species grows in a mass of free-standing branches likened to bunches of bananas.

3: **Bath sponge**
Spongia officinalis
Length: 35 centimetres
See above. This soft and porous sponge is grown commercially. It is sold to be used when bathing, thanks to its elastic skeleton.

4: **Stove-pipe sponge**
Aplysina archeri
Length: 1.15 metres
These long, purple cylindrical-shaped sponges grow in large groups of up to 22 tubes. They move to and fro with the current of the water.

5: **Orange fan sponge**
Stylissa flabelliformis
Length: 30 centimetres
This species is so called due to its resemblance to a Japanese hand-held fan. It grows on rocky shelves.

6: **Yellow finger sponge**
Callyspongia ramosa
Length: 30 centimetres
This sponge is found in waters around New Zealand. Its extracts are useful to the pharmaceutical industry.

7: **Venus's flower basket sponge**
Euplectella aspergillum
Length: 42 centimetres
The silicon spicules that form this sponge's skeleton fuse together to form a kind of natural glass, making it brittle and delicate.

8: **Purse sponge**
Grantia compressa
Length: 15 centimetres
This small and bulbous sponge is smooth and clean. It has an elongated neck, making it look like a gourd.

9: **Giant barrel sponge**
Xestospongia muta
Diameter: 2 metres
This slow-growing sponge can reach large dimensions, which suggests that it may live for a hundred years or more.

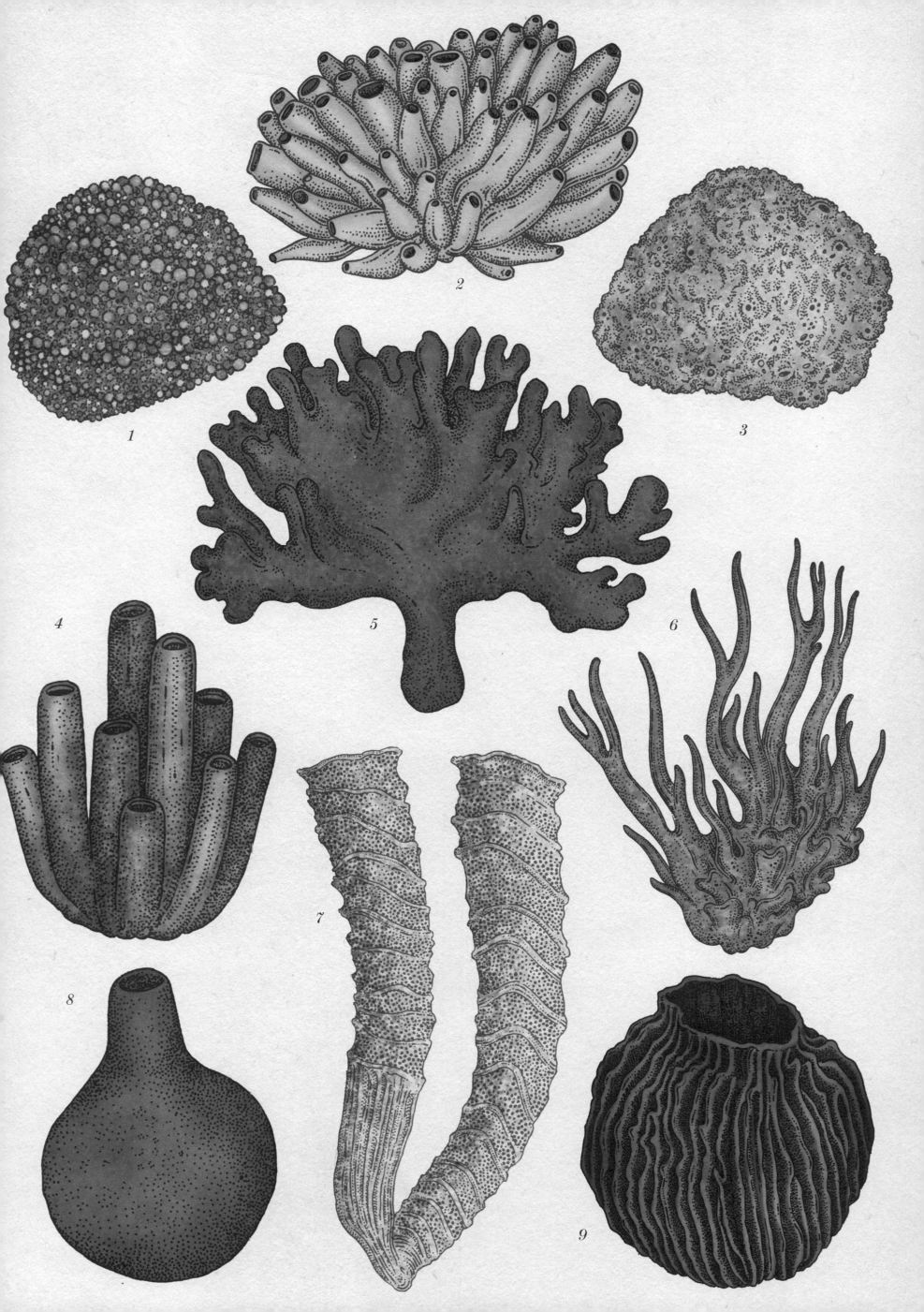

Cephalopods

The cephalopod family includes squids and octopuses, and is an ancient form of marine life that dominated the seas several million years before fish had evolved. There are now around 800 species of cephalopod, which can be found living in every ocean on Earth.

The word cephalopod means 'head-feet' in Greek, which reflects their anatomy. Their size is recorded by the length of their body cavity, called a mantle, which sits behind the head. Their large brains and advanced senses make them sociable creatures able to communicate with one another – they sometimes even shoal with fish for company.

Cephalopods can change the colour and pattern of their bodies to camouflage

themselves or ward off predators. They have sucker-like tentacles, and move by taking in water and shooting it out to move forward by jet propulsion.

Cephalopods produce ink and, when threatened, they release an inky cloud to confuse predators. Some can produce a ghost-like cloud a similar size, shape and colour to their own body, which acts as a decoy and gives the cephalopod a chance to escape.

Key to plate

1: Long-armed squid
Chiroteuthis veranyi
Mantle length: 12.5 centimetres
This slow-moving, alien-like squid lives at depths of up to 2.4 kilometres.

2: Whip-lash squid
Mastigoteuthis microlucens
Mantle length: 10 centimetres
The long, whip-like tentacles of this squid are covered in tiny, sticky suckers.

3: Angel octopus
Velodona togata
Mantle length: 16 centimetres
This deep-sea octopus lives at depths between 200–700 metres.

Cnidaria

There are over 10,000 known cnidarian species and they come in widely diverse forms. Some, such as sea anemones and corals (which are both anthozoans) are static polyps, which means they attach themselves to rocks. Others, such as box jellyfish, are free-moving, and contract their body shape to move.

Despite looking different, these species are uniformly aquatic and all have a decentralised nervous system, with no brain or heart. Also, all cnidarians have inherited a harpoon-like stinger from a single common ancestor. In fact, their name comes from the Greek word *knide*, which means 'nettle'.

Cnidarians are carnivorous, and kill and eat other animals in order to survive. Because they are not built to chase or hunt down their victims, they are known as 'passive predators' that wait for other creatures to blunder into them. When unwitting prey brushes past a cnidarian's tentacles, a hair-like trigger is activated, causing a toxic capsule to eject from its body and harpoon its victim. A cnidarian's sting can paralyse and kill its prey, and an unlucky encounter with the species can be extremely painful – and sometimes fatal – for humans, too.

Key to plate

1: Black sea nettle
Chrysaora achlyos
Diameter: 91 centimetres
This giant jellyfish occasionally rises to the ocean's surface in enormous groups known as blooms.

2: White-spotted jellyfish
Phyllorhiza punctata
Diameter: 47 centimetres
Rather than catching live prey, this jellyfish filters up to 50 cubic metres of seawater per day to extract nutrients.

3: Pacific sea nettle
Chrysaora fuscescens
Diameter: 27 centimetres
This jellyfish is covered in specialised stinging cells called nematocysts, which embed tiny thread-like barbs into their prey, paralysing it.

4: Dahlia anemone
Urticina felina
Diameter: 12 centimetres
This sea anemone has up to 160 short tentacles around its mouth for catching prey like shrimp and fish.

5: Staghorn coral
Acropora cervicornis
Height: 2 metres
The branches of this fast-growing coral are known to increase in length by 10–20 centimetres per year.

6: Brain coral
Diploria labyrinthiformis
Diameter: 2 metres
At night, this coral extends its tentacles to catch passing prey. During the day, it wraps its tentacles around itself for protection.

7: Stalked jellyfish
Haliclystus stejnegeri
Height: 15 centimetres
Rather than swimming freely like most other jellyfish, this species spends its entire life attached to rock or algae.

8: Blue button jellyfish
Porpita porpita
Diameter: 2.5 centimetres
Despite its name, this is not a jellyfish but a colony of zooids – tiny organisms, each of which have a unique job, like digestion.

9: Flowerpot coral
Goniopora djiboutiensis
Diameter: 1 metre
This coral is so-named because its polyps – with which it feeds – are arranged like the petals of a daisy.

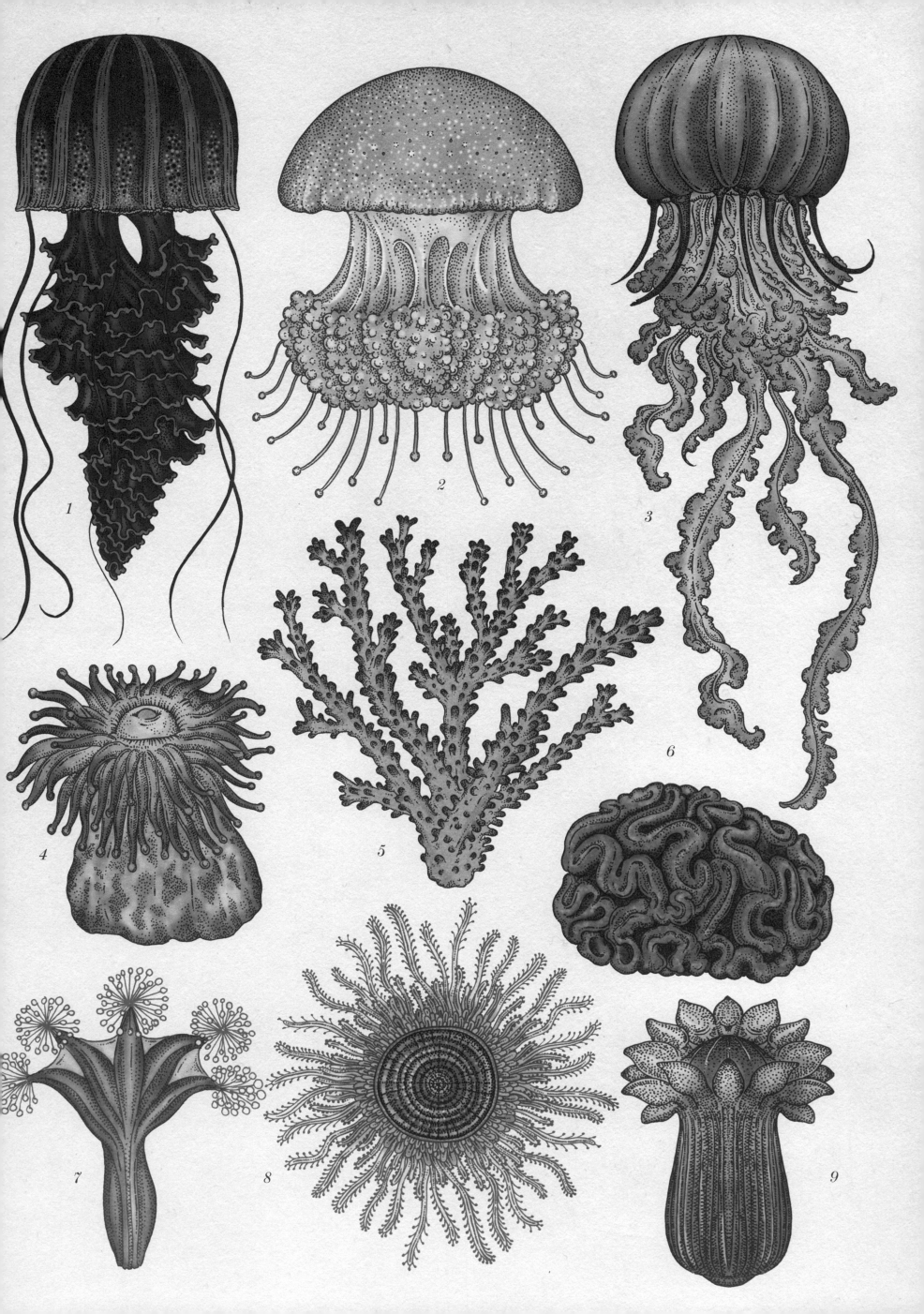

Flying Insects

Insects are an order of arthropod, making them closely related to crustaceans (crabs and lobsters), arachnids (spiders and scorpions) and myriapods (centipedes and millipedes). There are at least one million species of insects, together making up over 80 per cent of all living species on Earth. Around 10,000 new species of insect are identified every year.

All arthropods have segmented bodies, jointed limbs and exoskeletons, which are hard bodies with no internal bones. Although insects today are small in size, some prehistoric dragonflies grew to have wingspans of up to 70 centimetres.

They are the only invertebrates that have evolved to fly, and were the first herbivores on Earth, eating a diet of only plants. Over millions of years, plants and insects have co-evolved, with plants finding ways to defend themselves from being eaten by insects, while also relying on insects to spread their pollen to reproduce.

From birth, all insects experience a form of metamorphosis, gradually achieving maturity by undergoing a series of bodily changes. The changes experienced by the insect can be dramatic, with its body shape rendered almost unrecognizably different to its prior form. A well-known example is the transformation from caterpillar to butterfly.

--------------------------------- *Key to plate* ---------------------------------

1: Blue Mormon butterfly
Papilio polymnestor
Wingspan: 13 centimetres
This butterfly is common in heavy rainfall areas, such as evergreen forests.

2: Crane fly
Tipula paludosa
Wingspan: 4 centimetres
This nocturnal insect has long, delicate legs, which are easily detachable.

3: Mayfly
Ephemeroptera
Wingspan: 1.5 centimetres
Adult mayflies live for just one hour.

4: Emperor dragonfly
Anax imperator
Length: 7.8 centimetres
This species rarely lands, eating in flight.

5: Atlas moth
Attacus atlas
Wingspan: 30 centimetres
This moth has the largest wings of any insect, but no mouth to feed with.

6: Pale snaketail dragonfly
Ophiogomphus severus
Length: 5 centimetres
This species is rarely seen on cool days, preferring warmer temperatures.

7: Plains lubber grasshopper
Brachystola magna
Length: 5 centimetres
This species can jump over one metre.

8: Luna moth
Actias luna
Wingspan: 10 centimetres
This moth mimics fallen leaves.

9: Common green grasshopper
Omocestus viridulus
Length: 2 centimetres
The characteristic noise made by this grasshopper is the sound of the male rubbing its hind legs together to attract a female mate.

10: Common wasp
Vespula vulgaris
Length: 1.4 centimetres
When attacked, this aggressive wasp will send out an alarm to others to come and help.

11: Great black wasp
Sphex pensylvanicus
Length: 2.8 centimetres
This wasp paralyses its prey with its sting, then carries it to an underground nest to feed its young.

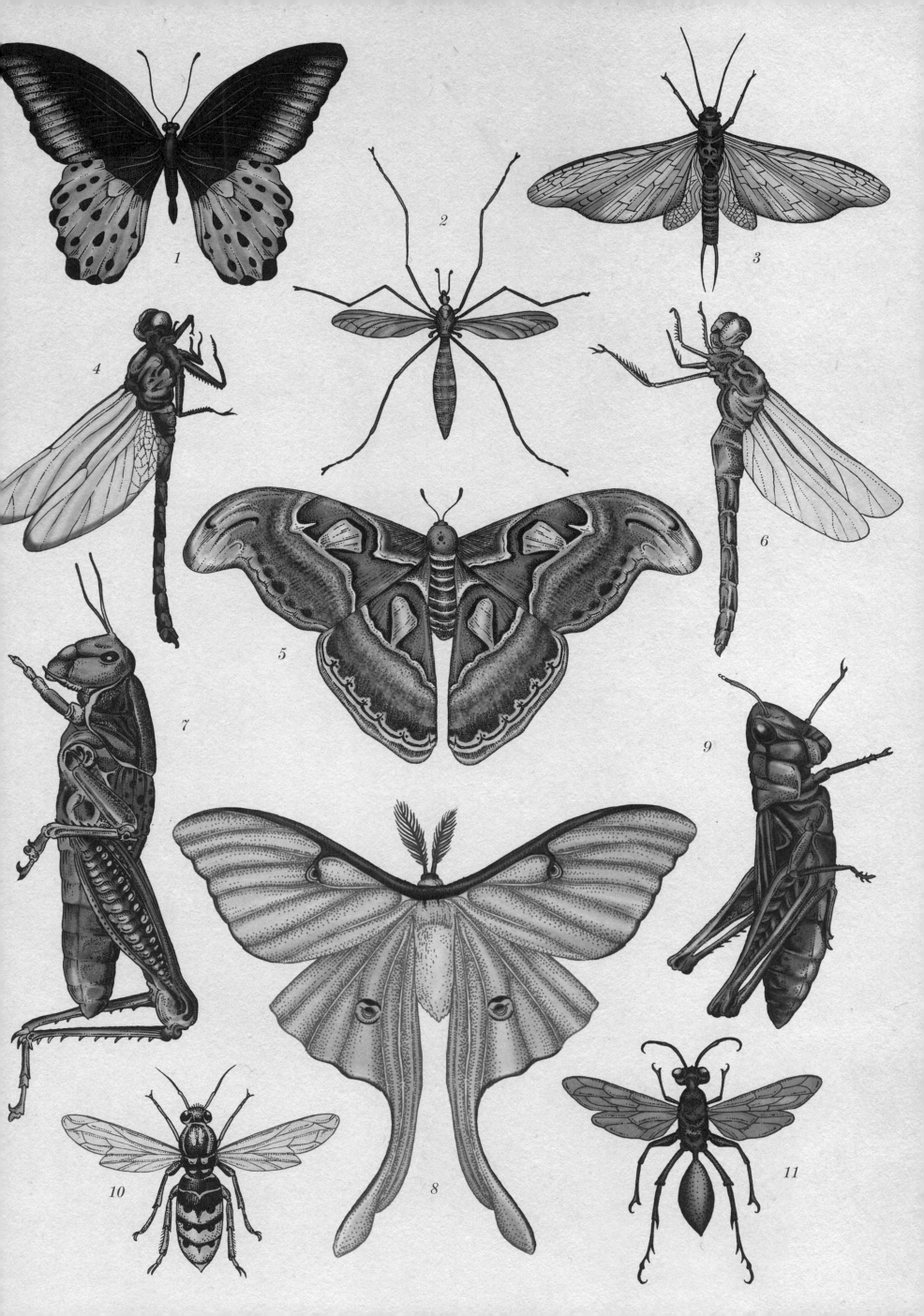

Habitat: Coastal Waters

Coastal habitats appear where the sea meets the land. There are about 356,000 kilometres of coastline around the world, and the conditions there vary depending on the local climate, landscape and turbulence of the ocean.

Coastal habitats are areas in constant flux as waves, tides and currents drag huge bodies of water across the shores, meaning there is continuous change to the landscape. However, rivers flooding into the sea, and the waves' erosion of the land provide a constant source of rich nutrients, and consequently life in coastal areas is the most abundant in the world.

Many of the creatures that live in coastal waters, such as crabs, limpets and scallops, are protected by hard shells, which help them to withstand battering waves. Some, such as mussels, are able to open their shells, sifting the water for food.

Some areas of the coast, known as intertidal zones, are above the water at low tide and below the water at high tide. This means that animals living in intertidal zones also face dramatic changes in temperature and varying water supplies, from fresh rainwater to saline seawater. Many species, such as barnacles, have cement glands that allow them to anchor themselves to a rock for stability as the tides rise and fall.

Key to plate

1: Northern short-fin squid
Illex illecebrosus
Mantle length: 14 centimetres

2: Crown jellyfish
Netrostoma setouchina
Diameter: 20 centimetres

3: Bushy-backed sea slug
Dendronotus frondosus
Length: 10 centimetres

4: Calico crab
Hepatus epheliticus
Width: 7.6 centimetres

5: Lettuce sea slug
Elysia crispata
Length: 5 centimetres

6: Blue mussel
Mytilus edulis
Length: 7.5 centimetres

7: True tulip snail
Fasciolaria tulipa
Length: 13 centimetres

8: Calico scallop
Argopecten gibbus
Length: 8 centimetres

9: Striped venus clam
Chamelea gallina
Length: 4 centimetres
Often found buried in muddy sand.

10: Little grey barnacle
Chthamalus fragilis
Diametre: 9 millimetres
Can be hermaphroditic (both male and female).

11: Cushion star
Oreaster reticulatus
Diameter: 24 centimetres
The juvenile is camouflaged green.

Fish

Fish

Fish were the first vertebrates to evolve from invertebrates. They are cold-blooded and live in nearly all aquatic environments: waters that are fresh, brackish or salty, freezing or tropical. With 32,000 different species, there is a broader diversity of fish than any other type of vertebrate. There are four categories of fish: ancient jawless fish, such as lampreys; cartilaginous fish, such as sharks; common ray-finned fish with bony skeletons, such as tuna; and lobe-finned fish, such as lungfish, which are thought to be the ancestors of all land-dwelling animals. These four groups show the various evolutionary stages that fish have gone through over millions of years.

Most species of the primitive jawless fish that once inhabited Earth are now extinct, but their notochord has an evolutionary legacy. This flexible rod down their back forms a kind of rudimentary backbone which bridges the gap between the spineless invertebrates and their bony vertebrate descendants on the tree of life.

Eventually, around 395 million years ago, some lobe-finned fish evolved into tetrapods. Tetrapods adapted to breathe air and inhabit land for the very first time in Earth's history. This evolutionary leap gave rise to amphibians, reptiles and, later, birds and mammals.

Key to plate

1: Red mullet
Mullus surmuletus
Length: 25 centimetres
This ray-finned fish is a species of goat fish, so called because of the two sensory barbels that hang from its chin, which it uses to locate prey. Its colour changes depending on its mood, its depth in the water and the time of day.

2: West Indian Ocean coelacanth
Latimeria chalumnae
Length: 153 centimetres
Known as the 'living fossil', this is the oldest-known living species of lobe-finned fish, and is closely related to the lungfish. The coelacanth was thought extinct until one was unexpectedly caught in 1938. It is nocturnal, and hides in caves throughout the day.

3: Sockeye salmon
Oncorhynchus nerka
Length: 28$^1/_2$ inches/72 centimeters
This adaptable species of ray-finned fish spends its early life living in freshwater lakes before swimming out into the saline waters of the Pacific Ocean. In order to spawn, it swims upriver to its birthplace.

4: Sea lamprey
Petromyzon marinus
Length: 60 centimetres
This ancient, primitive fish is jawless and appears to have evolved very little from the species that inhabited the seas 300 million years ago. It attaches itself to prey with its sucker-like mouth full of sharp teeth, and then draws out the flesh of its victim.

5: Atlantic mackerel
Scomber scombrus
Length: 30 centimetres
This ray-finned fish is the most commonly found species of mackerel in British waters. Fast and streamlined, this fish is known to perform long migrations. It forms huge shoals that swim close to the surface of the water.

6: Giant oarfish
Regalecus glesne
Length: 3 metres
This ray-finned fish is recorded as the longest species of fish in the *Guinness Book of Records*. It lives at depths of up to 1,000 metres and has been seldom observed alive. It is thought to swim by waving its body like a snake and rowing itself with its pelvic fins.

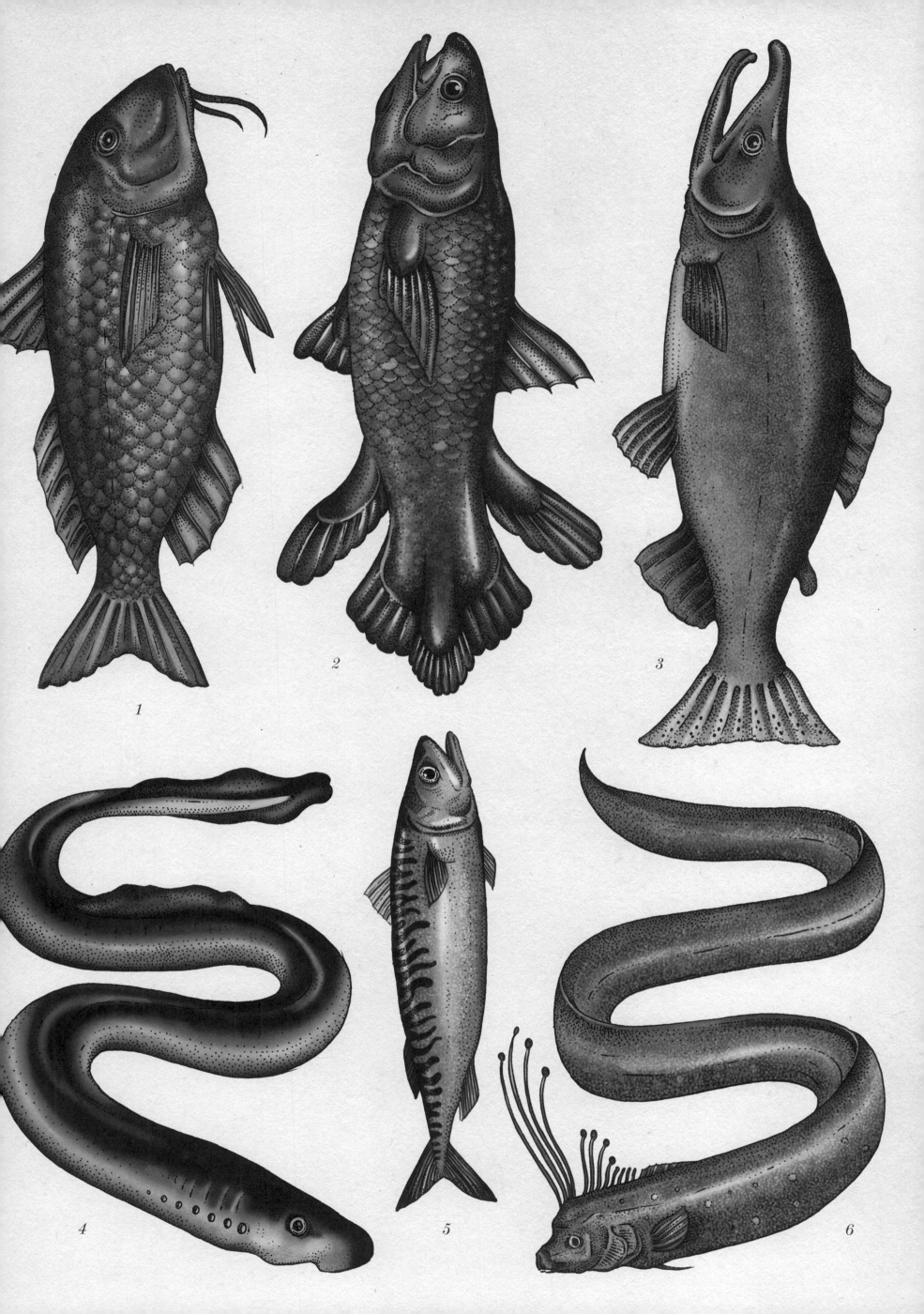

1

2

3

4

5

6

Sharks

Sharks evolved about 420 million years ago, and today there are more than 470 species, including the great white shark (*Carcharodon carcharias,* pictured below). It can grow up to 6.1 metres long, making it Earth's largest predatory fish. Sharks are cartilaginous fish: instead of hard bone, they have supple cartilage that makes their bodies lighter and more flexible.

Unlike other fish, sharks have rough skin with dermal denticles rather than smooth scales, and while many lay eggs, some give birth to live young. They do not have a gas-filled bladder to stay buoyant in water; instead, they rely on their oily liver and dynamic lift to stay at the right depth, cruising through water like birds do in air. This means that most sharks cannot move backwards, and that if they stop moving, they begin to sink.

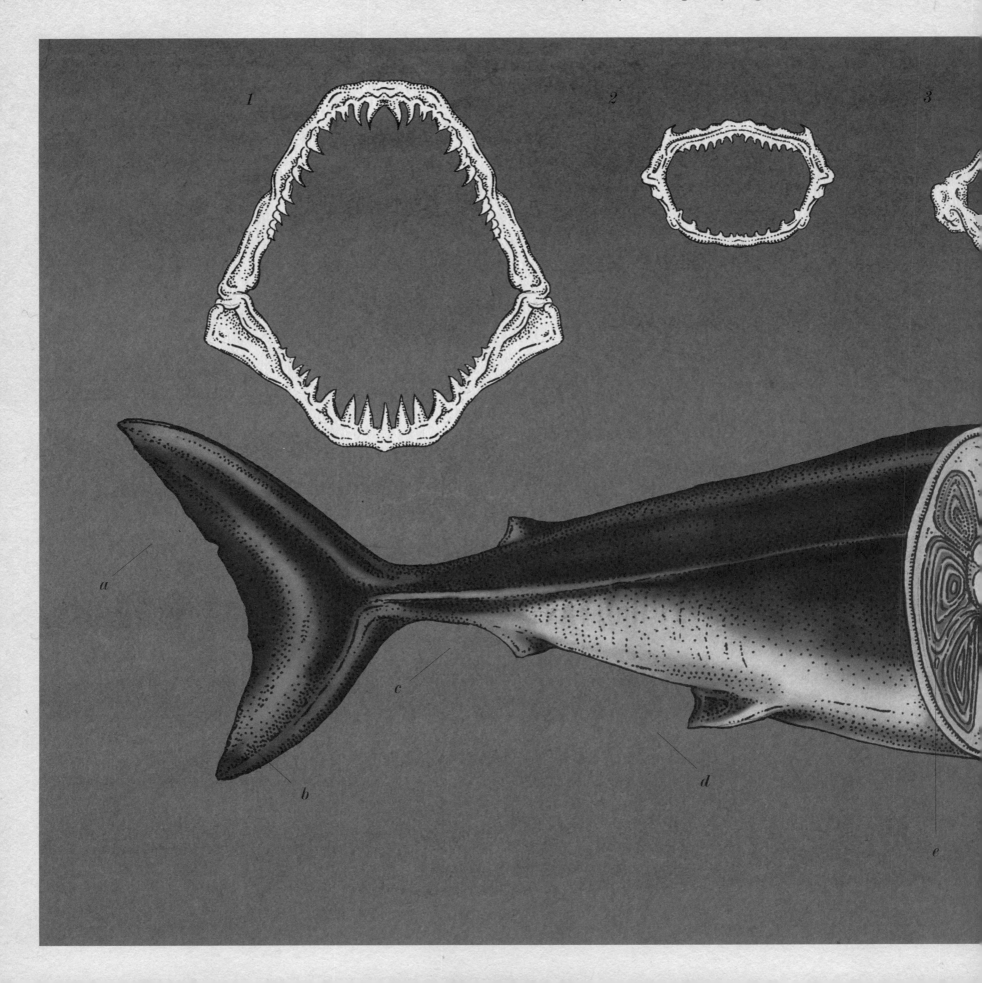

Sharks have very acute senses and can even detect the weak electrical signals emitted by their prey. This is called electroreception. Special blood cells keep their brain and eyes warm, giving them quick reactions. Their several sets of teeth constantly grow, moving forward and replacing blunted teeth with a new razor-sharp set waiting behind.

──────────────── *Key to plate* ────────────────

a: Upper caudal fin

b: Lower caudal fin

c: Anal fin

d: Pelvic fin

e: Spine

f: Pectoral fin

g: Gills

h: Jaw

1: **Shortfin mako shark's jaw**
Isurus oxyrinchus
Dagger-like teeth grip fast-moving prey

2: **Sharpnose sevengill shark's jaw**
Heptranchias perlo
Jagged upper teeth grip thrashing prey

3: **Zebra bullhead shark's jaw**
Heterodontus zebra

Adapted to feed from the seabed

4: **Kitefin shark's jaw**
Dalatias licha
Lower teeth form a continuous cutting edge to bite chunks from larger prey

5: **Sandbar shark's jaw**
Carcharhinus plumbeus
Adapted to a fish-based diet

Skates and Rays

Skates and rays are types of cartilaginous fish, making them younger relatives of sharks. They have long, thin tails which are often armed with a venomous sting, wide disc-like bodies, and 'wings' that they use to swim by beating them like a flying bird. Some species are commonly seen leaping out of the water.

To hunt, skates and rays hide on the seabed, waiting to ambush any small fish, mollusc or crustacean that crosses their path. A skate or ray will settle its broad, flat body – which is often covered with a camouflaging pattern – on the ocean floor, and flap its wings to stir up the sand, concealing itself. Underneath the sand, it breathes through spiracles behind its eyes. The fish cannot use its eyes to see when hiding in this way, so it uses its senses of smell and electroreception to locate and hunt prey.

Predators that hunt using electroreception are able to sense the weak bioelectric field generated by their prey's active nervous system. These electrical currents are extremely faint, but are easier to detect underwater than on land because water is a much better electrical conductor than air.

Key to plate

1: Thornback ray
Raja clavata
Length: 85 centimetres
This kite-shaped ray is one of the most commonly seen species, although identification can be difficult because colouration varies wildly from fish to fish. It has between 36 and 44 rows of teeth in its upper jaw, and its long, solid tail has thorns running down its length. Its eggs are encased in black leathery sacs, commonly known as mermaid's – or devil's – purses. It can live for up to twelve years.

2: Spotted eagle ray
Aetobatus narinari
Length: 180 centimetres
The spotted eagle ray is typically found in shallow tropical waters. It is also known to jump out of the water, sometimes inadvertently landing in boats. Its tail can grow more than three times its body width if left unharmed, but can easily get caught and damaged in fishing nets. This ray is ovoviviparous, which means that it gives birth to live young.

3: Blonde ray
Raja brachyura
Length: 100 centimetres
The blonde ray, named for its sandy colour, can be found throughout the waters of Europe and the Mediterranean, where it is most commonly found at depths of 350 metres. It has 60–90 rows of teeth and lives on a diet of small, bony fish and shrimp. It reproduces by laying horned black eggs, similar to those of the thornback ray.

4: Smooth skate
Malacoraja senta
Length: 59 centimetres
The heart-shaped smooth skate is a relatively small species, so named because, unlike other skates, its shoulders and upper pelvic fins are not covered with rough denticles. It can be found in the waters of the north-west Atlantic.

5: Shovelnose guitarfish
Rhinobatos productus
Length: 114 centimetres
The shape of the shovelnose guitarfish's dorsal fin initially led people to believe it was a shark, but it is in fact a species of ray. By day it lies on the ocean bed covered in sand, waiting to ambush a passing victim, and by night it cruises the seabed searching for prey.

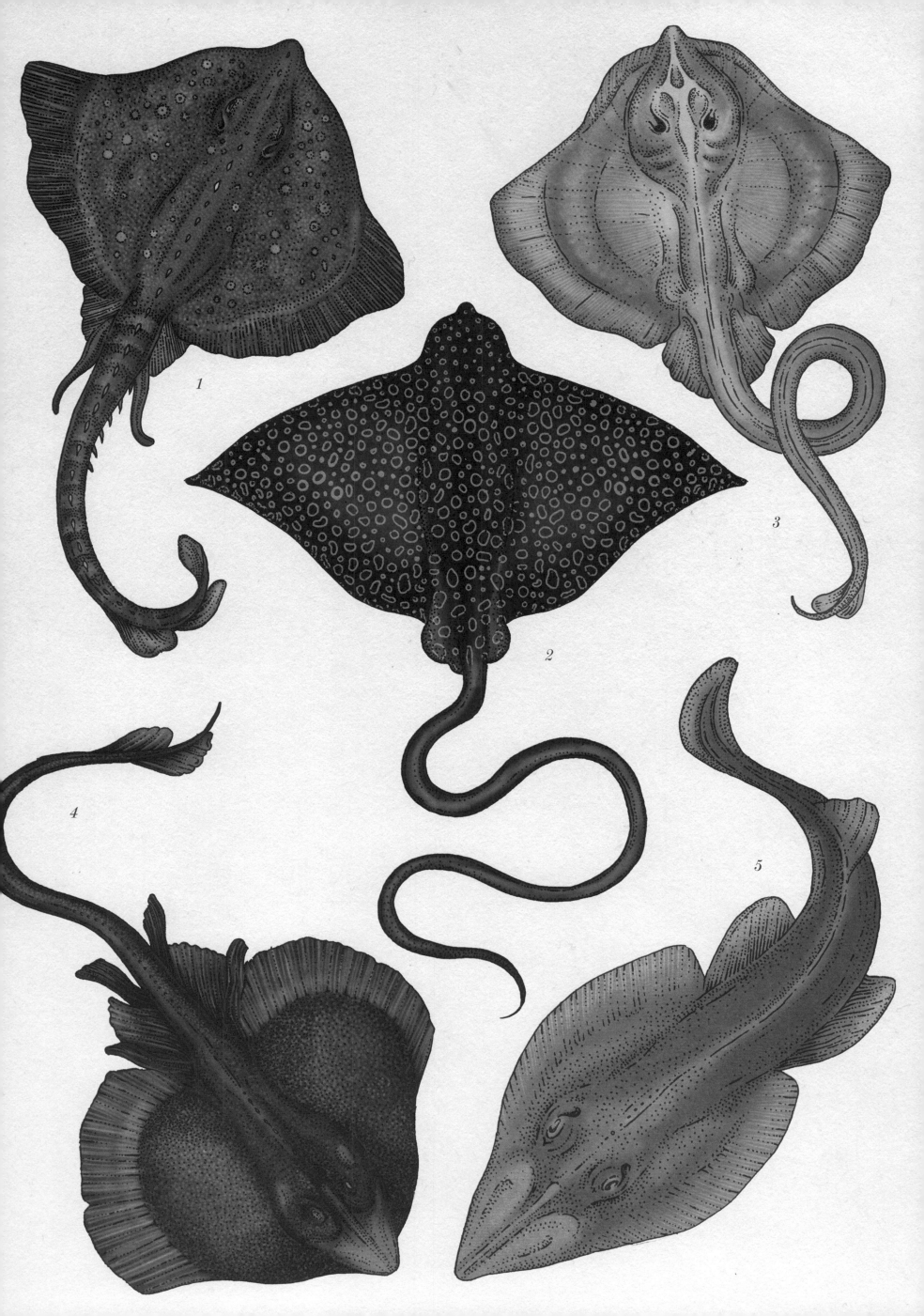

1

2

a

f

g

h

FISH

Ray-finned Fish

Ray-finned fish account for nearly 99 per cent of all species of fish. All have a jointed backbone: they were the first animals to benefit from this key evolutionary development. Their rayed fins – webbed skin supported by bony spines – allow them to make quick and complex movements, such as moving backwards, that cartilaginous fish cannot. They control their depth in the water with an air-filled bladder, which they use as a buoyancy aid. By adjusting the pressure of the gas, they can rise or sink.

Most of these species reproduce by laying eggs – sometimes laying millions at a time to increase the chances of some offspring surviving. For the same reason, ray-finned fish can often be found swimming together in their thousands, in large shoals which reduce an individual's risk of being eaten by a predator. Some shoals swim in a coordinated

movement known as schooling, a technique that has to be learned by young fish, who practise together in pairs. Schooling fish need to be able to see their neighbours clearly, and so they dissipate into normal shoals in the dark. Many species have marks on their bodies and tails known as lateral lines, which not only make them highly visible, but also enable them to detect changes in water pressure, helping them to remain at a certain distance from their neighbours.

Habitat: Coral Reefs

Coral reefs can be found in warm, clear, shallow parts of the ocean floor, and are colourful environments teeming with life. The reefs are hard, stony structures gradually formed over thousands – even millions – of years by tiny animals called coral polyps. Although they cover less than one per cent of the world's surface, these habitats support around 25 per cent of all marine species. The majority of shallow coral reefs are found in a wide band around the Earth's equator.

Coral reefs are sometimes called 'the rainforests of the sea' because of the rich biodiversity that flourishes in them. Over 4,000 species of fish can be found living in coral reefs, and they are among the most vibrant and varied species in the world. Their bright colouring helps the fish to camouflage themselves and confuse predators, and many keep to confined areas where they come to know every nook and cranny of the corals to hide in.

Many species of fish living in coral reefs have elongated snouts with which they probe into the coral polyps. Because they do not swim vast distances like open-water fish do, they have not evolved to be streamlined for moving through water for long periods of time. Instead, most have laterally flattened bodies that let them pass through confined spaces, and long ray-fins which give them the manoeuvrability to make sharp and quick movements in and out of the coral.

Key to plate

1: **Banggai cardinalfish**
Pterapogon kauderni
Length: 8 centimetres
This fish is most active in the morning, and feeds until sunset. Male and female cardinalfish form pairs that inhabit and defend particular territories.

2: **Mandarinfish**
Synchiropus splendidus
Length: 6 centimetres
This shy, slow and passive fish hides from predators in coral. If threatened, it can emit a bitter mucus with an unpleasant smell.

3: **French angelfish**
Pomacanthus paru
Length: 40 centimetres
Whilst the adult French angelfish is black and flecked with yellow, the juvenile fish has defined yellow bands, which fade as it ages.

4: **Stoplight parrotfish**
Sparisoma viride
Length: 30 centimetres
The parrotfish feeds in coral reefs throughout the day. At night, it creates a mucous sac that acts like a sleeping bag, so that predators cannot smell it.

5: **Clown anemonefish**
Amphiprion ocellaris
Length: 8 centimetres
This species lives in a harem of one female and several males. If the female dies, a male clownfish can change sex to take her place.

Gallery 3

Amphibians

Amphibians
Urodela
Frogs
Habitat: Rainforests

Amphibians

Amphibians take their name from the Greek word *amphibios*, meaning 'living both in water and on land'. They are famed for the dramatic metamorphoses they undergo in their lifetime. The first amphibians evolved around 370 million years ago from lungfish, and were the first quadrupeds, or four-footed creatures, to have jointed limbs. Approximately 10 million years later, unchallenged by predators, amphibians became the dominant animals on Earth. The climate – much warmer and swampier than today – suited them, and some amphibians grew to be bigger than crocodiles today.

Around 250 million years ago, however, reptiles began to rise in strength and number. Consequently, modern-day amphibians are much smaller and fewer, falling into three major orders: urodeles, caecilians, and frogs and toads. Most species today still have four limbs, although caecilians have adapted to their burrowing lifestyle by having strong skulls and no limbs at all.

Amphibians are cold-blooded, lay jelly-like eggs and tend to live in freshwater environments. Most have small, primitive lungs but are also able to breathe through their skin, which allows them to stay underwater without coming up for air. This means many amphibians can go dormant in winter, slowing their bodies and passing the colder months at the bottom of a pond or nearby water source.

Key to plate

1: Axolotl
Ambystoma mexicanum
Length: 20 centimetres
Also known as the Mexican walking fish, this species engages in a courtship display which involves dancing a 'waltz', followed by a 'hula', before copulation.

2: Mandarin salamander
Tylototriton shanjing
Length: 15 centimetres
This highly toxic amphibian is a relatively large and sturdy creature. It lightens in colour with age.

3: Darwin's frog
Rhinoderma darwinii
Length: 3 centimetres

Discovered by Charles Darwin in Chile, the male of the species has an oversized vocal sac in which it rears its young.

4: Allen's worm salamander
Oedipina alleni
Length: 13 centimetres
Endemic to Latin America, this species is so called because of its long, thin body. It has no lungs at all, breathing entirely through its skin.

5: Tomato frog
Dyscophus antongilii
Length: 10 centimetres
This frog, native to Madagascar, is nocturnal, burying itself in the moist

earth during the day and emerging to hunt at night.

6: Ornate horned frog
Ceratophrys ornata
Length: 18 centimetres
This unfriendly species has earned itself the nickname 'Pac-man' as a result of its enormous size and massive mouth, with which it ambushes victims.

7: White's treefrog
Litoria caerulea
Length: 9 centimetres
This adaptable species is commonly found in Australia. If threatened, it will emit a scream to scare away its potential predator.

AMPHIBIANS

Urodela

This family of amphibians includes salamanders and newts. Similar to other amphibians, they have smooth, moist skin, through which they absorb oxygen. (This is easier in cold water, which contains more oxygen than warm water.) This adaptation is so effective that some species have no lungs at all. Because their skin is delicate enough to allow oxygen to pass through, it is extremely sensitive to impurities, which makes them vulnerable to polluted water. This means that scientists often count the number of newts in an area to determine the health of the environment.

A male salamander can undergo changes during breeding season, which signal to females that he is ready to mate. The male Alpine newt, shown here, develops a crest that is re-absorbed into the body when mating has finished. Its skin also changes colour, from

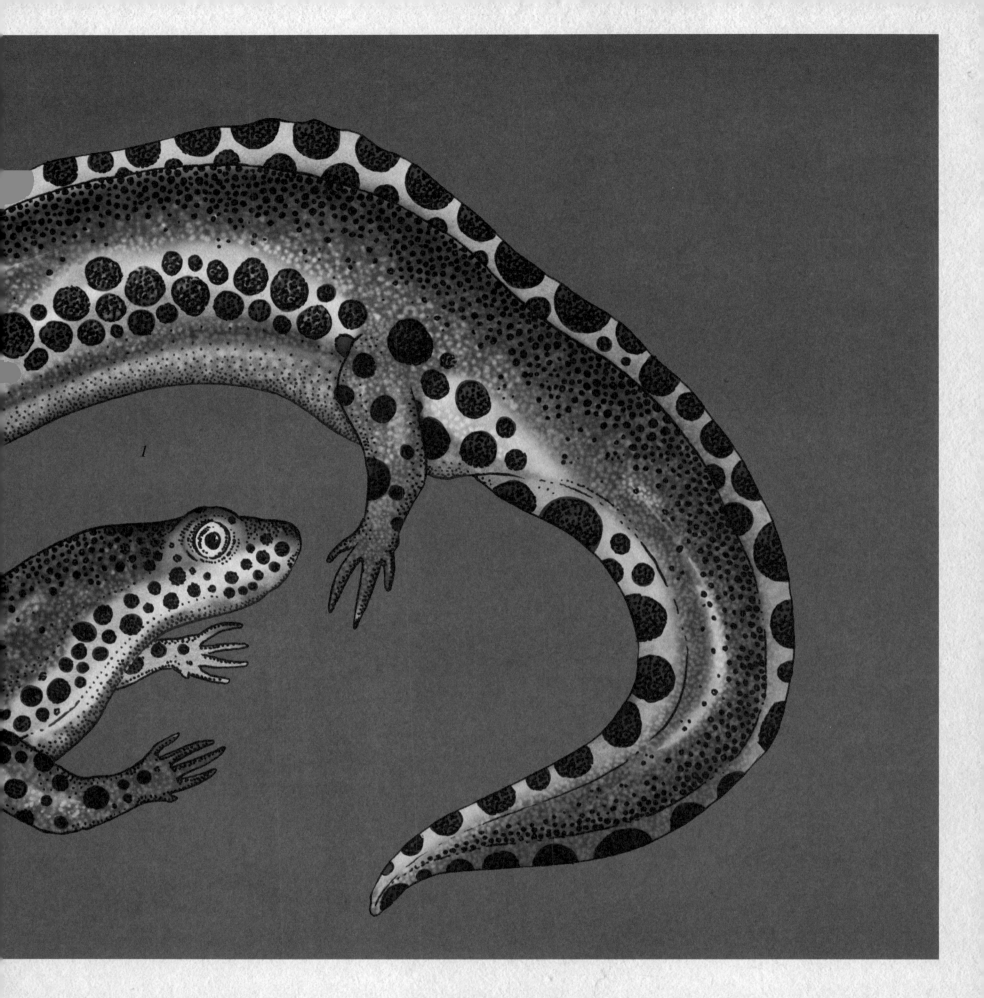

a camouflaging brown pattern to an eye-catching blue and orange. The eggs the female lays after mating do not have a shell, but instead are enclosed in a protective jelly.

Some salamanders are brightly coloured year-round. This warns predators that they are toxic and dangerous to eat. They have glands which produce a toxin so powerful that it could kill a human. These toxins, however, are for defensive purposes, and are only dangerous when ingested.

Another notable feature of salamanders and newts is their amazing ability to regenerate (or regrow) a lost limb!

--- *Key to plate* ---

1: Alpine newt
Ichthyosaura alpestris
Length: 10 centimetres
The Alpine newt lives in forested and mountainous terrains throughout central Europe, near to freshwater streams and ponds. It hibernates during the cold winter months and emerges in the spring, when it feeds at night. The male performs a tail-fanning dance for the female during courtship.

Frogs

An amphibian undergoes a radical series of transformations – known as a metamorphosis – during its life cycle. Its physical appearance changes dramatically during this time. Frogs experience a 'true' metamorphosis; most hatch from large batches of eggs laid in water and spend their first days as aquatic larvae known as tadpoles. These tadpoles have tails and gills that allow them to breathe underwater, and they have a vegetarian diet.

Soon after hatching, the tadpoles start to grow lungs, four legs and a large jaw, and their gills and tails disappear gradually in readiness for their move from water to land. Their eyes, tongues and legs grow bigger and – sometimes in the space of only a day – the tadpoles are transformed into insect-eating frogs.

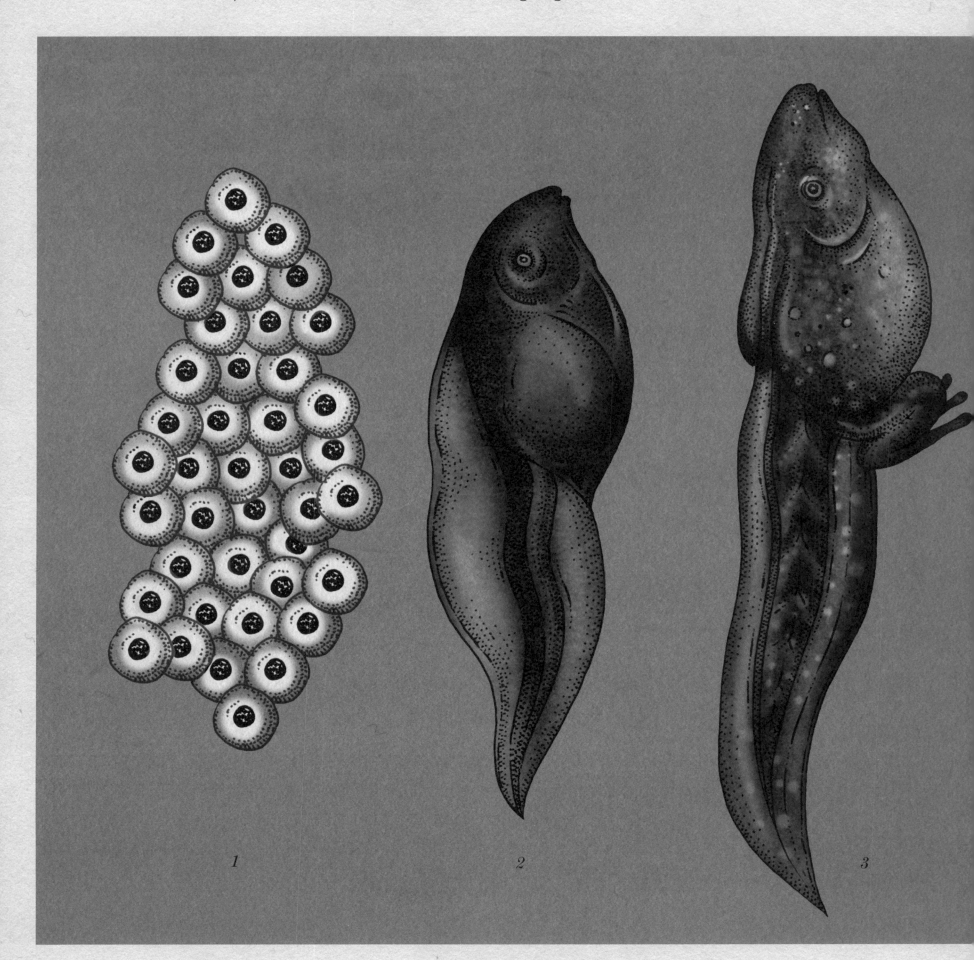

1 *2* *3*

Many species of frog have interesting ways of caring for their offspring. Some, such as the male Darwin's frog, nurture their young in their mouth, while others, such as the female pouched frog, allow their eggs to develop in a skin sac on their back for safety.

Most adult frogs have strong back legs that make them excellent at jumping and swimming, and some species have adapted to be able to climb and glide through the air. They develop good hearing and loud croaks, allowing them to communicate with one another across long distances, and their skins take on a distinctive colouring — either mottled and subdued to camouflage them, or bright and colourful to ward predators off.

Key to plate

European common frog
Rana temporaria
1: Frogspawn

2: Tadpole
3: Tadpole develops legs
4: Young froglet

5: Adult frog
After hatching, the development from tadpole to adult takes 12–16 weeks.

4

5

Habitat: Rainforests

Tropical rainforests are hot, humid areas, densely populated with trees and plants thanks to high levels of rainfall year-round. They are located around the equator, and are thought to contain more than half of the world's plant and animal species. Amphibians are particularly well suited to this habitat: there are more than one thousand different species of frog in the Amazon Basin alone. The frequent rains create a warm, swampy environment that allows amphibians' skin to stay moist (and therefore breathable) without having to stay close to ponds or rivers. As a result, many frogs are able to adopt lifestyles impossible elsewhere, living in trees and laying their eggs in leaves, safely out of reach of predators.

In order to travel from tree to tree, some frogs have developed the ability to glide. Using flaps of skin on their sides and between their toes, they stretch out as they fall through the air, allowing them to travel distances of up to 15 metres.

Some of the best-known species of frog, such as poison-dart frogs, live in rainforest habitats. Their brilliantly coloured skin warns predators of their deadly poison, which they are able to produce by eating toxic ants.

Key to plate

1: Blue poison-dart frog
Dendrobates azureus
Length: 4.5 centimetres
This species secretes poisonous toxins from glands all over its skin. It is aggressive and will fight off those that invade its territory. The male sings to attract a female to mate with.

2: Red-eyed treefrog
Agalychnis callidryas
Length: 6.4 centimetres
This species' namesake red eyes are thought to have adapted to its nocturnal lifestyle. It is an excellent climber thanks to suction cups on the underside of its feet.

3: Waxy monkey leaf frog
Phyllomedusa sauvagii
Length: 7.6 centimetres
This frog lays and sandwiches its eggs in a leaf above a pond. When the tadpoles hatch, they drop into the water. It coats itself in a water-repellent secretion to reduce water loss.

4: Granular poison-dart frog
Oophaga granulifera
Length: 2 centimetres
The male of the species is extremely territorial and establishes its breeding ground by calling incessantly. The calls attract potential mates and ward off other males.

5: Cerro Pando salamander
Bolitoglossa compacta
Length: 6 centimetres
This rarely seen salamander is moderately sized, with slightly webbed fingers and toes. It looks after its young for an unusually long period of time – up to eight months.

6: Thompson's caecilian
Caecilia thompsoni
Length: 1 metre
This limbless species is endemic to Colombia, and is the largest of the worm-like caecilians. It burrows with its hard skull and pointed snout. It is endangered due to deforestation.

Gallery 4

Reptiles

REPTILES

Gila Monster

Reptiles evolved from amphibians nearly 320 million years ago. They were the first animals to live land-based lives, which was possible thanks to scales that kept in their body moisture. Most adapted to lay shelled eggs, which sealed in water and allowed them to reproduce on land. Some species hatch these eggs internally and give birth to live young. Reptilian anatomy evolved to allow its species to walk more easily on land than amphibians – their name stems from the Latin word *reptilis* for 'creeping'.

Because of these adaptations, early reptiles had few predators and became a very successful class of animal. They grew huge in both size and number up to their apex of power as dinosaurs, which ended the amphibians' rule on Earth. For around 135 million years dinosaurs reigned over the animal kingdom, until a mass extinction around 65 million

years ago. After that extinction event, reptiles became smaller and fewer in number.

Modern reptiles share many characteristics with their dinosaur predecessors. They are cold-blooded and regulate their body temperature by moving between sun and shade. Many can shed and regenerate a limb, and some, such as chameleons, can even change colour. In the tree of life, they form an important evolutionary link – both birds, and later, mammals, evolved from reptiles. The evolutionary link is so close, in fact, that crocodiles are more directly related to early kinds of bird than they are to lizards!

Key to plate

1: Gila monster
Heloderma suspectum
Length: 56 centimetres
The Gila monster, a species of venomous lizard which lives in North America, spends most of its time

underground. It feeds mostly on eggs and small creatures often found newly-born in nests, and only eats between five and ten times a year in the wild – but when it does, it devours up to one third of its body mass.

a: Gila monster's skull and teeth
Unlike venomous snakes, which have hollow fangs, Gila monsters have very large, grooved teeth in their lower jaw. As they bite into their prey, poison travels down the grooves.

Turtles, Tortoises and Terrapins

Turtles are members of an order of reptiles called Testudines, which also includes tortoises and aquatic terrapins. This name refers to the hard shell that all its species possess, as a *testudo* in ancient Rome was a hard screen or shield that soldiers used to protect themselves. Little of the modern turtle's anatomy has changed from its prehistoric ancestors', who date back more than 220 million years, making turtles and tortoises more ancient than all snakes, lizards and crocodiles.

Turtles' shells are attached to their bodies, and so their protective armour can never be taken off or left behind. Land-dwelling tortoises have higher, domed shells, whilst aquatic species have flatter shells. To hide inside their shells, some species fold their head alongside their shoulder, whilst others retract their neck and head backwards. Box turtles have a hinged bony plate that allows their shells to close completely.

Males will often perform elaborate courtship rituals to impress females, who lay shelled eggs after mating. The temperature that the eggs are kept at affects the sex of the hatchlings (a trait shared with crocodiles and some lizards).

Key to plate

1: **Green sea turtle**
Chelonia mydas
Length: 150 centimetres
This large sea turtle is a herbivore, feeding mostly on seagrasses. Populations of green sea turtles can be found in tropical waters of the Atlantic and Pacific oceans.

2: **Painted turtle**
Chrysemys picta bellii
Length: 25 centimetres
Also known as the firebelly turtle, this species spends long hours basking in the sun, particularly early in the day. It is common sight to find several painted turtles piled on top of one another on a log.

3: **Blanding's turtle**
Emydoidea blandingii
Length: 20 centimetres
This turtle has a plastral hinge that forms a protective hatch at the front of its shell. It is omnivorous, feeding on a range of foods such as berries, fish and frogs.

4: **Diamondback terrapin**
Malaclemys terrapin
Length: 15 centimetres
The mild-mannered diamondback terrapin lives in brackish lagoons, tidal marshlands and sandy beaches in east-coast America. The species nearly became extinct due to over-hunting and destruction of its habitat.

5: **Leopard tortoise**
Geochelone pardalis
Length: 50 centimetres
The leopard tortoise is a large tortoise found in savannah habitats in Africa, where it can live for up to 100 years. Its grasping toenails make it an agile walker, strong swimmer and surprisingly good climber.

6: **Indian star tortoise**
Geochelone elegans
Length: 28 centimetres
The Indian star tortoise has a high tolerance of water, and so can be found in places that experience monsoon seasons. Its dome shape allows it to easily self-right.

Snakes

Snakes are characterised by their lack of limbs and their long, tube-like bodies. They are believed to have descended from lizards, losing their limbs in the process of evolution. Because of their narrow body shape, their paired organs, such as kidneys, are stacked one in front of the other rather than side by side, and most have just one lung. Their long and flexible backbone allows snakes an exceptional dexterity of movement.

There are around 3,400 species of snake, and they can be found on every continent except for Antarctica. All are carnivorous and possess large, flexible jaws, which allow them to eat prey much larger than their own heads. Because their teeth are designed for killing, but not chewing, they swallow their victims whole. Sometimes a snake's meal can be seen to travel down its body as it digests.

Snakes have a strong – and directional – sense of smell, and use it to track prey with their forked tongues. Different species have their own methods of attack; around one in ten species has a venomous bite, delivered with poisonous fangs, whilst others use constriction, crushing prey to death by coiling their bodies around their victims.

Key to plate

1: Arizona coral snake
Micruroides euryxanthus
Length: 0.5 metres
This snake can be found in scrubby, arid regions of North America. Its colourful bands warn others that it is a venomous species. In fact, its venom, which it delivers with its fangs, is similar to a cobra's.

2: Paradise treesnake
Chrysopelea paradisi
Length: 1.2 metres
Living in the forests of South-East Asia, the paradise treesnake is an adept climber. This snake has the ability to glide from tree to tree by flattening its body and launching itself into the air from a high branch.

3: Blood python
Python curtus brongersmai
Length: 1.5 metres
Found in tropical swamps around Indonesia, the non-venomous blood python gets its name from its deep red colouration. When incubating her eggs, the female coils around them and shivers her body to keep them warm.

Crocodiles and Alligators

Crocodiles and alligators are called crocodilians as a group, and are related, having emerged around 140 million years ago from common ancestors who managed to survive extinctions that other reptiles, such as dinosaurs, did not. These ancestral forebears were fearsome predators, growing up to twice the length of today's crocodiles and alligators.

The modern species that populate Earth now share their ancestors' body shape and large, fearsome jaws, containing numerous teeth. They are good swimmers, reaching speeds of more than 30 kilometres per hour in the water. Crocodilians are carnivorous animals and will hunt any kind of animal on land or in water. Because their jaws are designed to tear meat apart (rather than chew it), they will clamp large prey, such as a wildebeest, in their jaws and perform the 'death roll', spinning prey underwater until a piece of meat comes off.

The name *crocodile* comes from the ancient Greek word *krokodilos*, meaning 'worm of the stones', whilst the word *alligator* derives from the Spanish term for lizard, *el lagarto*. They are sociable and vocal, and can often be found grouped together and communicating with one another on riverbanks or in freshwater lakes. Female crocodilians make fierce mothers and will guard their young for up to two years.

Crocodilians have superior senses, including night vision, and receptors along their jaws that allow them to sense prey moving in water. A flap of tissue in their throats acts as a valve, allowing it to breathe whilst partly underwater by closing off its respiratory system. Because their eyes, ears and nostrils are situated on the very top of their heads, they can submerge themselves in water in order to ambush prey. Their ears are so sensitive that they can hear calls from their unborn young still inside their eggs.

Key to plate

1: **Nile crocodile**
Crocodylus niloticus
Length: 5 metres
The Nile crocodile is the second largest reptile on Earth and has a reputation as a fearsome man-eater. It is thought that up to 200 people are killed by Nile crocodiles each year.

The Nile crocodile is predominantly nocturnal, and it can sometimes be found escaping the extreme heat of the midday sun in underground burrows. Alongside other crocodilians, it has evolved to have advanced flexibility in its hip and ankle joints, giving it good mobility on land.

a: Skull
b: Shoulder bone
c: Humerus
d: Carpus and ulna
e: Ribs
f: Fibula and tibia
g: Femur
h: Caudal vertebra

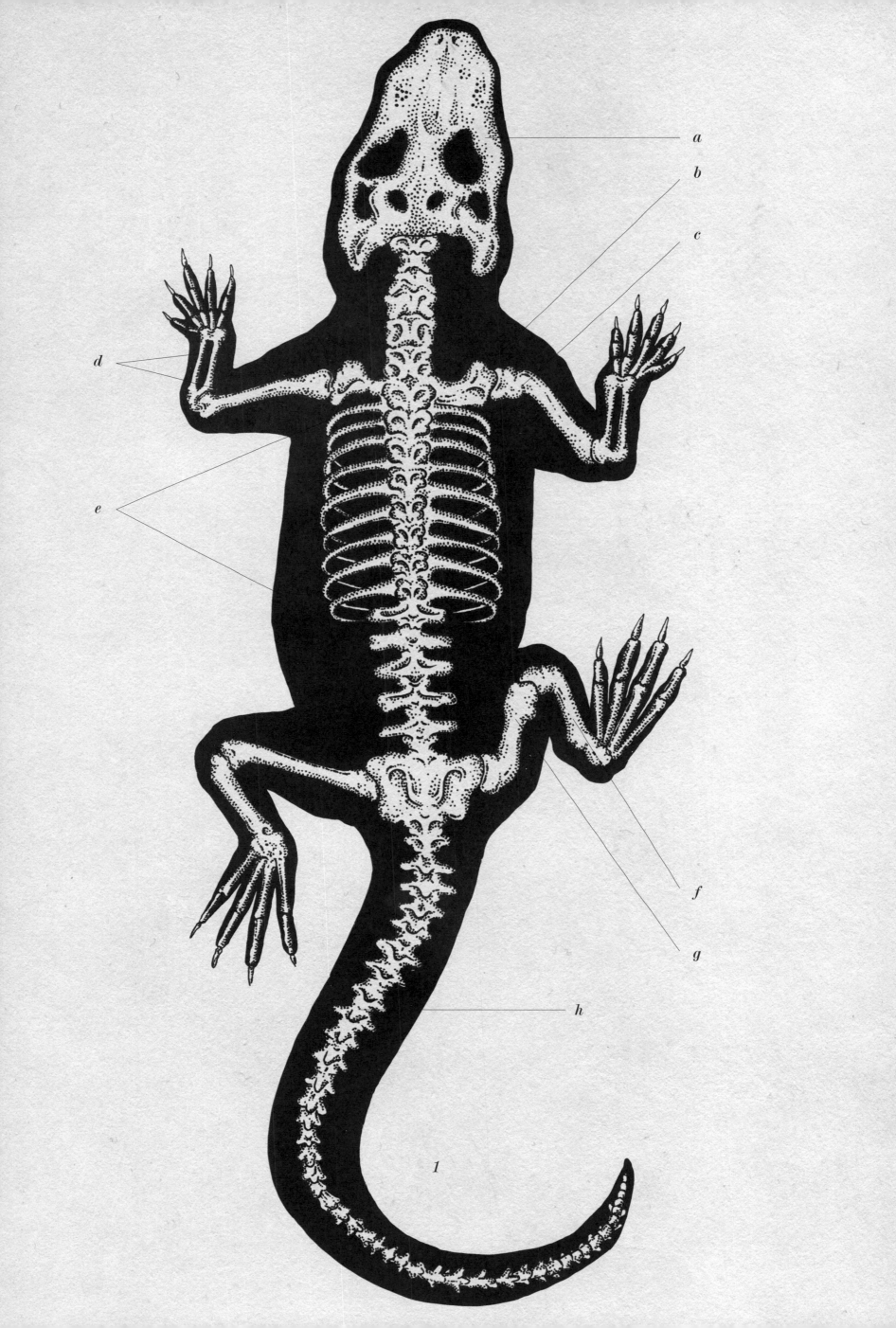

a

b

c

d

e

f

g

h

1

Habitat: Deserts

Deserts are areas defined by an extremely dry climate, where very little rain falls and very few plants are able to grow. Some deserts are cold, mountainous and barren, but the largest deserts in the world are in areas where the sun is extremely hot, such as the Sahara Desert in Africa. Even in deserts that experience scorching heat by day, the temperatures can plummet at night, meaning that any species living in these habitats must cope with extreme changes in temperature.

The great highs and lows in temperature mean that rocks weather quickly, breaking down into fine sands. Because of these arid conditions, few plants are able to survive and take root, which means there is little vegetation to hold the ground together. The sands, therefore, are easily blown around, and sometimes form sand dunes that are sculpted by winds, creating a constantly changing landscape.

Reptiles are especially suited to living in these environments because they are able to survive with little water. Many lizards gape their mouths open when basking in the hot sun to release heat. Because they cannot sweat to cool themselves, they take shelter beneath a rock during the hottest parts of the day and emerge to hunt in the evening when the sun begins to set and the sands retain enough heat to keep the animal warm. To catch prey, many hide under the sands to ambush a passing victim.

Key to plate

1: Desert kingsnake
Lampropeltis getula splendida
Length: 1.2 metres
Although this is a non-venomous species of snake, it is able to consume other toxic creatures such as rattlesnakes. When threatened, it will flip onto its back and lie motionless, playing dead.

2: Baja California collared lizard
Crotaphytus vestigium
Body length: 9 centimetres

This creature hibernates under a rock in the cold winter months and becomes active in the warmer seasons. When running, it can become bipedal, standing up on its two hind legs.

3: Black tailed rattlesnake
Crotalus molossus
Length: 97 centimetres
This creature is so named due to the warning sound it makes by shaking its tail when threatened. The venom it injects with hollow fangs stops its

victim's blood from clotting, causing the prey to bleed to death.

4: Western banded gecko
Coleonyx variegatus
Body length: 10 centimetres
This secretive creature is nocturnal, and hunts insects, arachnids and baby scorpions by night. If threatened, it can curl its tail over its head to mimic a scorpion. If caught, it can detach its tail altogether from its body, which gives it a chance to escape.

Birds

Flightless Birds

Early birds evolved from tree-dwelling dinosaurs around 150 million years ago. Along with their sister group, the order Crocodilia, they were the only members from this branch of the tree of life to survive the mass extinction that killed the dinosaurs around 65 million years ago. Like ancient reptiles, early birds were carnivorous. They have since diversified wildly and can now be found on every continent and habitat on Earth.

All birds are warm-blooded, with two legs, two wings that evolved from the reptile's forelimbs, feathers, beaks and a lightweight skeleton. Like reptiles, birds reproduce sexually and lay hard-shelled eggs, from which a chick hatches.

Linking reptiles to modern birds on the tree of life are a group of primitive

species called the Palaeognath, which are land-dwelling, predominantly flightless, birds. Their name comes from the Greek term for 'old jaws', referring to their reptile-like mouths, which betray their reptilian ancestry along with their bare, scaly legs.

———————————— *Key to plate* ————————————

1: **Common ostrich**
Struthio camelus
Height: 2.4 metres
This is the largest and fastest-running bird on Earth. It can reach speeds of up to 70 kilometres per hour thanks to its powerful long legs, which can stride up to 4.9 metres. Ostriches have been known to kill lions with their kick!

2: **Southern cassowary**
Casuarius casuarius
Height: 1.7 metres
The cassowary is recognisable thanks to its horn-like casque and two red wattles that hang from its throat. It has a dagger-like claw on its inner toe, with which it defends itself, charging down and spearing its target.

3: **Cassowary eggs**
Length: 13.8 centimetres
Unusually, the male cassowary incubates the egg and raises its young alone.

4: **Ostrich egg**
Length: 15 centimetres
The largest egg of any bird. All hens lay their eggs in the dominant hen's nest.

Penguins

Penguins can be found in coastal areas in the Southern Hemisphere and are instantly recognisable thanks to their upright stance and distinctive black and white plumage. Whilst easy to spot on land, their colouring acts to camouflage them in water: their black backs match the ocean's darkness from above, and their white bellies blend in with the brightness of the sun and ice from below. This is known as countershading.

Ungainly on land and completely flightless, penguins are fast and agile swimmers, with large webbed feet, and wings that have adapted to act like flippers in the water. It is thought, however, that their ancestors could indeed fly, and that penguins are in fact more closely related to the albatross than to other flightless birds.

Most species have evolved to survive in cold and harsh environments. Their feathers, densely packed and waterproof, offer excellent insulation, and their blood flow has adapted so that they do not freeze when standing on ice. Incubating an egg in these conditions is challenging, and to do this they lay a single egg, warming it under their plumage and keeping it off the ice by balancing it on their feet. They are attentive parents, taking turns catching fish and feeding their young once hatched.

Key to plate

1: **Emperor penguin**
Aptenodytes forsteri
Height: 1.1 metres
The emperor penguin is the largest of all the species of penguin. It lives in Antarctica, which is one of the most inhospitable climates on Earth.

It is a highly sociable creature and lives in huge colonies around the South Pole which number tens of thousands of birds.

In order to stay warm, it huddles in a group with other emperor penguins. Each member of the group takes turns to stand exposed to the cold winds on the outside of the cluster before rotating back inside the centre for warmth.

Its diet primarily consists of fish, which it hunts in the sea. It has been known to travel distances of more than 1,000 kilometres in a single foraging trip! Its body is streamlined for swimming and its feathers are covered in a waterproof oil, which keeps it dry and warm in the water.

Underwater, the emperor penguin can stay submerged for up to 18 minutes at a time. Its skeleton has evolved to be solid, rather than air-filled like other birds – this allows it to dive to depths of up to 450 metres without suffering from barotrauma, a lethal condition brought on by changes in pressure, which cause pockets of gas within a creature's body to expand and cause damage to the surrounding tissue.

The emperor penguin is famous for its reproductive cycle. It chooses to breed during the Antarctic winter between May and June, when no other creature inhabits the region, thus reducing the threat of predators.

The penguins walk distances of up to 80 kilometres inland, where the female lays her egg. She transfers it to her male partner, who incubates it in his brood pouch, balancing it on his feet. The female then departs, leaving the male to protect the egg from winds as fierce as 190 kilometres per hour and temperatures as low as -40°C. He survives this time without food, living on stored body fat alone. Once the chick has hatched, the female returns with food for her young, releasing the male to return to the sea to feed. By this time, he will have fasted for more than three months.

1

Albatrosses

Learning to fly was a key evolutionary step for most birds, and scientists still aren't sure how or why they first took to the skies. Nevertheless, it has allowed them to inhabit every continent, habitat and island on Earth. Flying birds' bodies have adapted to become perfectly suited to the task, with light skeletons made up of air-filled bones. Their long, hinged wings are covered in aerodynamic feathers, and their strong pectoral muscles allow them to flap their wings, pushing the air downwards and generating lift.

Albatrosses are known for their masterful flying, and spend most of their lives gliding above the seas, only coming back to shore in order to nest. They have the largest wingspan of any living bird and they use this to great effect, soaring through the skies and scouting for fish with their powerful sense of smell.

3

To help sustain their long flights, albatrosses are especially reliant on gliding, which allows them to conserve energy. The way they stay aloft is similar to the way that aeroplanes fly — long, curved wings slice through the air at speed, making the air particles travel faster across the top of the wing than underneath it. This creates a lower air pressure above the bird than below, which keeps the bird aloft.

Key to plate

1: Wandering albatross
Diomedea exulans
Wingspan: 3 metres
This is the largest species of albatross and is found almost exclusively south of the equator. The chicks are born with brown plumage and turn increasingly white with age

2: Black-browed albatross
Thalassarche melanophrys
Wingspan: 2.2 metres
The young black-browed albatross has a blue beak that turns orange in adulthood. A salt gland in its nasal passage allows it to excrete any excess salt from seawater out of its body.

3: Waved albatross
Phoebastria irrorata
Wingspan: 2.25 metres
This is the only albatross species found entirely in the tropics. It can spend six years at sea before returning to land to mate. It feeds at night, when squid swim close to the surface of the water.

Flamingos, Storks, Ibises and Herons

With elongated legs and necks, these creatures tend to live in wetlands and are generally carnivorous, living on a variety of aquatic prey. They can be found inhabiting areas across the globe, and some species are partially migratory.

Flamingos are highly sociable creatures and live together in enormous flocks. They benefit from the vigilance of their neighbours, who keep a lookout for predators, and often rear their young together in crèches. Whilst they may look decorative, they have adapted to survive in challenging environments and tend to inhabit lakes with high levels of salt or alkalis in the water. Their characteristic colouring derives from a type of bacteria they ingest when eating their diet of shrimp. Consequently, flamingos can range in colour from off-white to a shocking coral pink. Usually, the healthier the animal, the more vibrantly coloured it is, which makes its hue attractive to a mate.

Related to flamingos are storks, herons and ibises. Herons in particular are excellent fishermen: standing still and silent, they wait for prey. They have lightning-fast reactions and employ their S-shaped neck and sharp bill to spear fish with impressive speed.

Key to plate

1: **Grey-winged trumpeter**
Psophia crepitans
Height: 52 centimetres
Named for its loud honking call, this easily tamed bird makes a good guard.

2: **American flamingo**
Phoenicopterus ruber
Height: 109 centimetres
The flamingo buries its head to feed, sucking and filtering mud with its beak.

3: **Northern gannet**
Morus bassanus
Height: 91 centimetres
This bird dives into water from heights of up to 40 metres to catch fish.

4: **Brown booby**
Sula leucogaster
Height: 74 centimetres
This seabird tracks tuna from the sky to catch small fish that flee to the surface.

5: **Western reef heron**
Egretta gularis
Height: 65 centimetres
During courtship, this heron's dark legs take on a pinkish-red colour.

6: **Black-crowned night heron**
Nycticorax nycticorax
Height: 62 centimetres
This nocturnal hunter is the most widely distributed heron in the world.

7: **Grey-crowned crane**
Balearica regulorum
Height: 105 centimetres
This species is well-known for its elaborate courtship ritual, where it dances to impress a mate. It lives in the dry African savannahs, but returns to water during the breeding season.

8: **Goliath heron**
Ardea goliath
Height: 142 centimetres
This is the largest and tallest species of heron on Earth, and is able to walk in deeper waters than its competition, spearing prey with its sharp bill. It is commonly found in sub-Saharan Africa.

Birds of Prey

Birds of prey are also known as raptors, which comes from the Latin word *rapere*, meaning 'to seize'. They are carnivorous, and most have evolved into formidable hunters. Many are apex predators, meaning that they are at the top of the food chain, with no predators of their own. Some, such as the bald eagle, are so fearsome that they will hunt mammals comparatively larger than themselves, like small deer. Others, such as vultures, are scavengers, and eat the flesh of animals that are already dead, called carrion, rather than hunting live prey.

Birds of prey have acute senses, sharp beaks for tearing apart flesh, and strong feet that usually feature long talons with an opposable hind claw for snatching their target from the air. They are exceptionally long-living birds, some reaching 50 years of age.

Birds of prey are typically fast and agile flyers: the peregrine falcon reaches the fastest speed of any living creature on Earth by ambushing its prey from high in the air and diving towards its target at speeds of up to 389 kilometres per hour. The highest flying species of bird is also thought to be a bird of prey: the Rüppel's vulture has been known to reach altitudes of up to 11,000 metres.

Key to plate

1: **Secretary bird**
Sagittarius serpentarius
Wingspan: 2.1 metres
The secretary bird, endemic to Africa, is one of the only birds of prey known to chase its prey down on foot. It has also been observed flushing out its victim by stomping on clumps of vegetation and then going in for the kill, with repeated strikes from its hard beak or blows from its strong feet. When attacking snakes, the bird uses its wings to protect itself from a venomous bite.

2: **African harrier-hawk**
Polyboroides typus
Wingspan: 1.6 metres
The African harrier-hawk is omnivorous, eating a varied diet of fruits and berries as well as small

vertebrates. It hunts mostly in trees and bushes, and seldom in flight. It is good at climbing, and uses its wings and double-jointed legs to scramble up trees to raid other birds' nests.

3: **Ornate hawk eagle**
Spizaetus ornatus
Wingspan: 1.3 metres
The ornate hawk eagle lives in the tropical forests of Central and South America. It can often be seen perched high at the top of a tree, scanning the ground below for prey. It hunts other birds, reptiles and mammals, and has even been known to attack primates.

4: **Crested caracara**
Caracara plancus
Wingspan: 1.2 metres
The crested caracara is found in

open land from the southern parts of North America down to Peru and Amazonian Brazil, and is a common sight on cattle ranches. It is not an agile flyer and seldom hunts for prey, opting instead to scavenge for food and feed on carrion.

5: **Bateleur**
Terathopius ecaudatus
Wingspan: 1.7 metres
The bateleur is endemic to Africa. It has a unique style of flying: it rocks its wings from side to side as it glides, as though it were trying to balance. The skin on the bateleur's face and legs shows how it is feeling, and flushes bright red when it gets agitated. It can also puff out its crest and chest feathers, and emit a barking noise uncommon among other raptors.

Exotic Birds

Birds in tropical and exotic environments often display bright and colourful plumage. Birds-of-paradise are among the most vibrant and elaborate creatures on Earth, and during the breeding season the males perform elaborate courting rituals before prospective mates, displaying their decorative feathers and dancing to impress the female.

Birds are warm-blooded creatures with a fast metabolism, which has allowed their brains to evolve into a more advanced state than those of their reptilian forebears. Some species, such as macaws, are considered particularly intelligent, and have been known to employ logical thought in using tools to access food that is out of reach. They are social creatures, and many parrots form pairs that share a strong bond.

Hummingbirds are some of the smallest birds in the animal kingdom, measuring less than 13 centimetres long. However, they display a formidable dexterity and precision when flying, being the only birds able to fly backwards. Hummingbirds are also able to hover in one spot in order to extract nectar from flowers. They accomplish this by flapping their wings up to 80 times a second, which creates their distinctive 'hum'.

Toucans are known for their large and colourful bills. These bills are far from solely decorative, however. They use them to reach many fruits in a tree without needing to fly to a different branch. Their bills also help them to regulate their body temperature.

Key to plate

1: **Ruby-throated hummingbird**
Archilochus colubris
Length: 9 centimetres
Although the hummingbird is specially adapted to feed on nectar, it raises its young on insects, which are a better source of protein.

2: **Greater bird-of-paradise**
Paradisaea apoda
Length: 43 centimetres
This is the largest species of bird-of-paradise, famous for its elaborate ritual mating dance in which it displays its colourful plumes.

3: **Ruby-topaz hummingbird**
Chrysolampis mosquitus
Length: 8 centimetres

This species can be found in tropical South America. Its bill, compared to other hummingbirds, is relatively short.

4: **Rose-ringed parakeet**
Psittacula krameri
Length: 40 centimetres
The rose-ringed parakeet has the widest distribution of any parrot species: it is found from West Africa, to South-East Asia, to areas in Europe.

5: **Rosy-faced lovebird**
Agapornis roseicollis
Length: 18 centimetres
Native to south-west Africa, this sociable bird can often be spotted sleeping with its face turned towards its neighbour.

6: **Mallee ringneck parrot**
Barnardius barnardi macgillivrayi
Length: 33 centimetres
The smallest and least aggressive of the Australian ringneck parrots, the mallee can live for more than 15 years.

7: **Red-breasted toucan**
Ramphastos dicolorus
Length: 43 centimetres
This is the smallest of the toucan family. Despite its large size, its bill is relatively light.

8: **Galah**
Eolophus roseicapilla
Length: 35 centimetres
This species is one of the most common cockatoos in Australia.

Owls

There are two types of owl: typical owls and barn owls. Both are carnivorous and have evolved to hunt in the dark. They have distinctive round, flat faces with small beaks and large eyes that allow them to see well in poor light. Owls are masters of the surprise attack – their feathers are camouflaged to blend in perfectly with their surroundings in dim conditions, and are adapted to muffle the sound of their wings, making them near-silent flyers.

Owls have eyes that are located at the front of their head, giving them two overlapping fields of vision. This means that they can accurately determine their exact distance from their prey, but the unusual size and shape of their eyes means that owls cannot move them in their sockets, like humans do. As a result, owls have developed flexible necks in order to turn their heads and change their view – some can rotate their head up to 270 degrees!

Owls also have an extremely acute sense of hearing thanks to a pair of ears that are located at slightly uneven heights on either side of their heads. This asymmetrical placement allows the owl to discover the exact direction a sound is coming from. Their directional hearing is the most accurate of any animal species.

Key to plate

1: **Barn owl**
Tyto alba
Wingspan: 108 centimetres
The barn owl is the most common of all species of owl, and can be found on every continent except for Antarctica. Its name comes from its tendency to adopt man-made buildings, and it can be found living in both urban and rural environments.

It has excellent night vision and directional hearing which allows it to detect creatures hidden from sight underground or beneath snow – a useful ability that allows it to hunt in deepest winter.

When breeding, the female takes sole responsibility for incubating the eggs, during which time the male hunts and delivers meat and grubs to her.

2: **Spectacled owl**
Pulsatrix perspicillata
Wingspan: 84 centimetres
Found primarily in the rainforests of Central and South America, the spectacled owl is named for its dramatic white eyebrows which frame its eyes, resembling a pair of glasses.

It is an unsociable creature, roosting alone in a tree by day and hunting by night. It is most vocal under the cover of darkness and makes a distinctive knocking or tapping sound.

The female spectacled owl emits a high-pitched scream which has been likened to a steam engine.

It feeds on insects, birds and amphibians, and will occasionally hunt larger creatures such as skunks, possums and other small mammals.

3: **Southern white-faced owl**
Ptilopsis granti
Wingspan: 68 centimetres
This small – and rarely seen – species of owl is found in a variety of habitats in sub-Saharan Africa, from woodland to open savannah.

It has been nicknamed the 'transformer owl' thanks to the unique displays it puts on when threatened. If approached by an opponent slightly bigger than itself, it puffs up its feathers, attempting to seem larger. However, when faced with a much greater predator, it flattens and sucks its feathers into its body, hides behind its wing and squints its eyes, to camouflage itself against a tree.

It occupies other birds' nests and will even evict the current occupants!

Habitat: Woodlands

Woodland habitats are made up of trees, shrubs and grasses; the greater the variety of plants growing, the more animals it can support as a habitat. Some woodlands are deciduous, meaning that the trees change with the seasons, shedding their leaves in the winter and growing new foliage in the spring. Others are evergreen, keeping their leaves (or 'needles') year-round.

Many species of bird live in woodlands for some – or all – of the year. Some of the world's best-known songbirds can be found in this habitat, and although they can be difficult to spot, you can tell them apart by their complex and unique songs. Birds sing for lots of reasons: to assert their territory, attract a mate or alert others to danger.

In areas where the woodland is deciduous, many species take part in an annual migration. They live and breed among green trees during the summer, then fly thousands of kilometres south when the weather turns colder and the leaves begin to fall to find food and warmer weather. This is a dangerous and exhausting journey, so most birds travel in large flocks, seeking safety in numbers.

Key to plate

1: Stock dove
Columba oenas
Length: 33 centimetres
Doves and pigeons belong to the same family. The stock dove is the largest of all doves, and is the rarest and most geographically dispersed.

2: Eurasian blackbird
Turdus merula
Length: 24 centimetres
This is a species of thrush and is a partial migrant: many choose to stay during winter. It can send alternate sides of its brain to sleep during flight.

3: Eurasian nuthatch
Sitta europaea
Length: 15 centimetres
This species' name derives from its habit of wedging nuts into gaps in trees before hacking them open.

4: House sparrow
Passer domesticus
Length: 16 centimetres
The house sparrow is a very sociable bird known to share dust baths and indulge in social singing. It coexists happily alongside humans.

5: European starling
Sturnus vulgaris
Length: 22 centimetres
The starling is a gregarious bird that lives in huge, noisy flocks. It is well known for its beautiful flocking displays at sunset.

6: Song thrush
Turdus philomelos
Length: 23 centimetres
The song thrush, named for its melodious voice, eats snails by smashing their shells with a stone. It migrates at night by cover of darkness.

7: Blue tit
Cyanistes caeruleus
Length: 12 centimetres
The small blue tit lives on an insect-based diet. The yellowness of its belly indicates the number of yellow and green caterpillars it has eaten.

Mammals

Marsupials

Mammals are the most recent animals to appear on the tree of life. They evolved from reptiles, and egg-laying monotremes, like the duck-billed platypus, provide the evolutionary link between these two classes of animal. Today, mammals dominate life on Earth.

Mammals have hair or fur and are warm-blooded, which allows them to maintain a constant body temperature in any climate. They give birth to live young, which they feed with their own milk. Most have four limbs, a tail, and a relatively large brain, which allows some species the benefit of unprecedented mental capacity and complexity of thought. Developing high levels of intelligence takes time and experience, and so mammals rely on their nurturing parents for a comparatively long time as they grow.

Marsupials are pouched mammals and can be found in Australasia and the Americas. Their young are born at an earlier developmental stage than other mammals and are initially carried in the mother's protective pouch. As mammals were evolving, Earth's landmasses were gradually moving into the positions where our continents are located today. Marsupials were originally found in South America around 50 million years ago, but they travelled to Antarctica by land, from where, at that time, Australia was only a short stretch of water away. Since then, Australia has been geographically isolated, which explains why the mammals found there today are so unique.

Key to plate

1: Red kangaroo
Macropus rufus
Length without tail: 123 centimetres
The largest species of marsupial, this kangaroo is robustly built, with a tail strong enough to support its entire body weight. To avoid overheating in the hot Australian sun, it licks its wrists.

2: Striped possum
Dactylopsila trivirgata
Length without tail: 26 centimetres
This nocturnal creature forages for grubs and probes for termites with its elongated fourth claw. It drums bark with its feet to locate hidden wood-boring insects. Like a skunk, it can emit a foul stench when threatened.

3: Common spotted cuscus
Spilocuscus maculatus
Length without tail: 40 centimetres
Whilst the male is rust-coloured and spotted, the female has plain creamy fur. This shy nocturnal creature lives in the tropical rainforests and dense mangroves of Australasia, and is almost completely arboreal, equipped with strong grasping fingers and toes for a life in the trees.

4: Sugar glider
Petaurus breviceps
Length without tail: 18 centimetres
This small, softly furred possum has a thin membrane that stretches from its wrist to its ankle, which acts as a parachute, allowing it to glide from tree to tree. Its long, bushy tail helps it to balance and direct itself in mid-air, and its large claws give it excellent grip.

5: Koala
Phascolarctos cinereus
Length without tail: 74 centimetres
This creature spends most of its life in the trees, out of danger from predators. Its diet of eucalyptus leaves is so poor in nutrients that a koala spends much of its day conserving energy, sleeping. The leaves are highly fibrous and difficult to digest, and so noxious that a mother feeds her young on her own faeces, having filtered out the dangerous toxins they contain.

Elephants

Elephants were once part of a much larger family that also included mammoths, but currently all but two kinds are extinct. These surviving species of elephant are now also threatened by humankind's poaching of their ivory and destruction of their habitats.

On the tree of life, elephants are most closely related to manatees, and it is thought that millions of years ago they lived predominantly in water, using their trunks as snorkels. Even today, they remain strong swimmers.

Elephants are instantly recognisable thanks to their unique and flexible trunks, which they use to grab and hold objects with, their long, sharp tusks, and their large, flat ears. Overheating is a problem for elephants, as they have not evolved to sweat like other mammals. To counter this, if an elephant begins to overheat, blood travels to its ears. They

flap their ears in the breeze to cool the blood, which then circulates back through its body, keeping the elephant's temperature down.

Elephants are now the largest animals living on land. To help support their massive bulk, their legs are positioned straight underneath their bodies. Despite their size and weight, they are surprisingly quiet when walking, thanks to shock-absorbing tissues in their feet, which also help them remain sure of foot.

Key to plate

1: Asiatic elephant
Elephas maximus
Height: 2.6 metres
The Asian elephant has smaller ears, smaller tusks – if it has any at all – and a back more arched than its African cousin's. A female Asian elephant is

ready to breed at around 14 years of age, and she carries her unborn calf for up to 22 months. The newborn is dependent on its mother for up to 48 months – which means that the female elephant is only able to reproduce once every three or four years.

This species has teeth that move forward inside its mouth as it ages, which is unusual for a mammal. These wear down with use and are replaced by the set behind. However, with only limited sets available, if all its teeth are used in its lifetime, it can starve.

Primates

Primates are thought to have evolved between 65 and 85 million years ago. They are made up of two groups: the mostly nocturnal Strepsirrhini, which includes lemurs, lorises and bushbabies, and the Haplorhini, which includes apes, monkeys and *Homo sapiens* (human beings). The word *primate* derives from the Latin word *primas*, meaning 'of the first rank', while *Homo sapiens* derives from the Latin for 'wise man'.

Primates have four limbs, each with five digits, and most have a tail, providing extra stability in the treetops. Their forward-facing eyes help them to judge distances when swinging from branch to branch and, unlike most other animals, primates can see a large spectrum of colour. They are most notably characterised by their large brains, which make them highly intelligent and sociable.

About 2.3 million years ago, primates began to stand and walk on two feet. They displayed a highly developed intellect through their use of tools and ability to create fire. Modern humans evolved around 200,000 years ago, which makes us one of the youngest and newest species on Earth. The earliest modern human beings were found in south-western Africa, and people all over the world share a common ancestry with our forefathers there.

Key to plate

1: **De Brazza's monkey**
Cercopithecus neglectus
Length: 62.3 centimetres
This Old World monkey is endemic to the forests of central Africa. Its large, robust feet allow it to roam the forest floor more successfully than other primates. It is sociable and communicative, imparting information visually, vocally and via touch.

2: **Golden lion tamarin**
Leontopithecus rosalia
Length: 33 centimetres
This New World monkey lives primarily in the trees, eating flowers, nectar and eggs. It forms strong bonds with members of its group and is known to share its food and care for another's offspring.

3: **Guereza**
Colobus guereza
Length: 58 centimetres
This mantled guereza is found in equatorial regions of Africa and lives in groups of up to 15 individuals. It spends the majority of its time in the branches of trees, but can come down to the forest floor to feed. At night, a sentry keeps watch for predators.

4: **Mandrill**
Mandrillus sphinx
Length: 80 centimetres
The playful mandrill is one of the largest species of monkey in the world, and lives in the tropical rainforests of Africa. It spends its days foraging on the forest floor, returning to the trees to sleep.

5: **Common chimpanzee**
Pan troglodytes
Length: 135 centimetres
The highly intelligent chimpanzee is one of humankind's closest relatives, and shares 98 per cent of our genes. It lives in groups of up to 150 individuals, in forested regions of Gabon, Cameroon and the Democratic Republic of the Congo.

6: **Black-crested mangabey**
Lophocebus aterrimus
Length: 55 centimetres
The black-crested mangabey, found in Angola and the Democratic Republic of the Congo, has a distinctive 'whoop-gobble' call with which it defends its territory. Deforestation has placed this species under threat.

Rodents

Rodents are an extraordinarily successful kind of mammal; they have flourished in wildly different environments and can be found in vast numbers all around the world. Counting rats, mice, squirrels, hamsters, porcupines and beavers amongst their ranks, they make up around 40 per cent of all mammal species.

Some rodents, such as mice, are prolific breeders, which partly explains why there are so many of them on Earth! They become sexually mature early in their lives, and are able to reproduce year-round. They have short gestation periods, give birth to multiple live young, and have to wait only a short period of time for their young to become

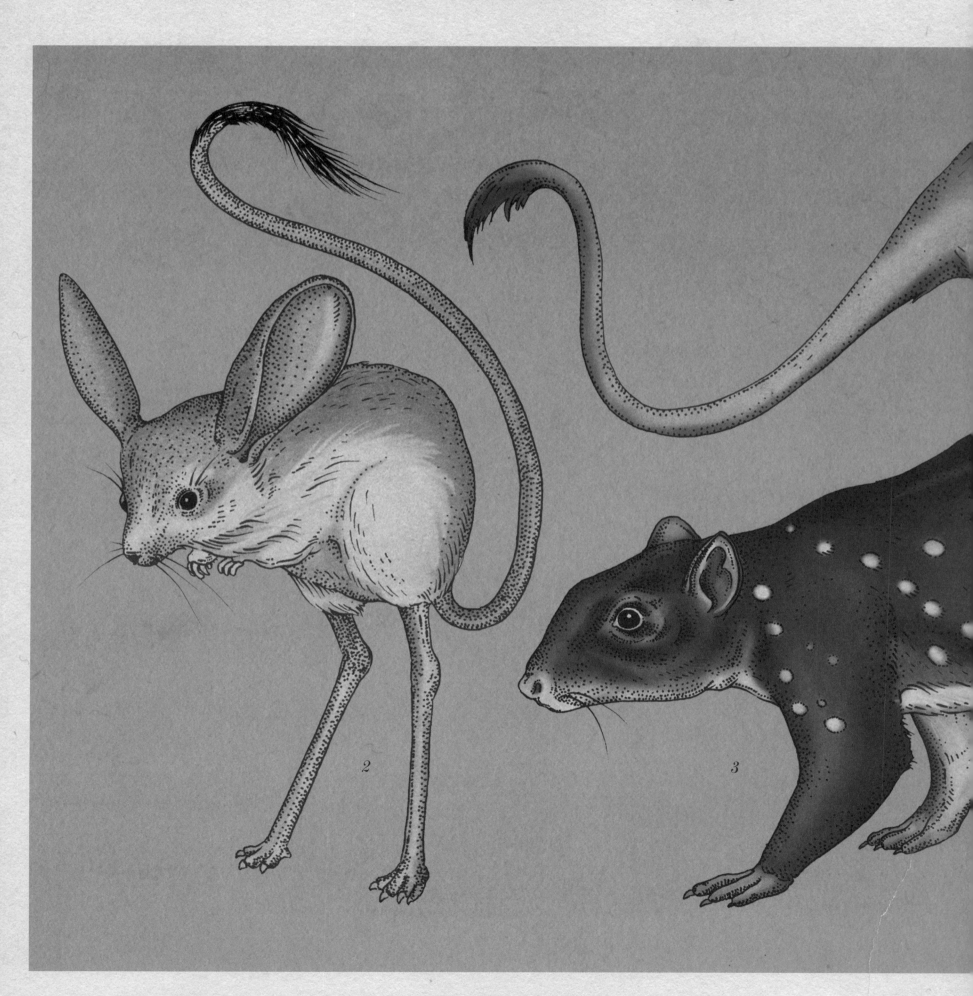

independent before they are able to mate again. Therefore, it is possible for one mouse to give birth to over 100 young in a single year!

All rodents have sharp front teeth that never stop growing, which means that they need to frequently gnaw on things to stop them from growing too long.

─────────────────── *Key to plate* ───────────────────

1: **Northern Luzon giant cloud rat**
Phloeomys pallidus
Length without tail: 40 centimetres
This Philippine rat lives in the treetops.

2: **Long-eared jerboa**
Euchoreutes naso

Length without tail: 8 centimetres
Native to the Gobi Desert, this rodent performs high leaps to catch insects.

3: **Lowland paca**
Cuniculus paca
Length without tail: 70 centimetres

Paca means 'alert' in the Tupi language spoken in Brazil where this species lives.

4: **Prevost's squirrel**
Callosciurus prevostii
Length without tail: 24 centimetres
This squirrel lives in Asian rainforests.

Bats

Bats are the only mammals to have evolved to fly. Skin stretched across their forelimbs and down their extended digits forms wings, which are much thinner than those of birds and allow bats to manoeuvre more quickly and accurately in the air.

Bats are mostly nocturnal creatures, sleeping through the day, often wrapping their wings around themselves for warmth. They come out to hunt at twilight when there is less competition from other predators for the same food sources. They eat a variety of things, including a large quantity of insects, and sometimes – in the case of the vampire bat – they even suck blood from large mammals, such as a sleeping cow.

Bats can detect prey and navigate in complete darkness thanks to echolocation, an ability they share with some other mammals such as dolphins and whales. They build a detailed image of their surroundings by sending out high-pitched sound pulses and deducing from the time that noise takes to echo back what is located nearby. When it rains, however, the falling raindrops interfere with the sound pulses, meaning they cannot navigate by echolocation, so they do not come out to hunt.

Key to plate

1: **Indian flying fox**
Pteropus giganteus
Wingspan: 135 centimetres
This nocturnal mega-bat, also known as the greater Indian fruit bat, can be found in tropical regions of south-central Asia. It rests in trees with several hundred fellow bats. The height of a male's position in a tree can indicate his hierarchical position within the group.

2: **Brown long-eared bat**
Plecotus auritus
Wingspan: 23.5 centimetres
This species is commonly found in the UK and across mainland Europe. Its ears match its body in size, giving it an excellent sense of hearing that helps it to locate moths, earwigs and other insects in the dark. It has adapted to roost in small colonies in man-made buildings as well as trees.

3: **Seba's short-tailed bat**
Carollia perspicillata
Wingspan: 30 centimetres
Found in the forests of Central and South America, this gregarious bat lives in colonies of up to one hundred individuals. It eats several varieties of fruit and is an important distributor of seeds, dispersing up to 2,500 per night in its droppings. When food is lacking, it falls into a sleep-like state of torpor.

4: **Diadem roundleaf bat**
Hipposideros diadema
Wingspan: 50 centimetres
This is the most commonly found species of the Old World leaf-nosed bats, found from Australia to south-east Asia. It roosts in caves and hollow trees, and hunts by hanging from a perch and snatching large passing insects, such as moths.

5: **Yellow-winged bat**
Lavia frons
Wingspan: 35.6 centimetres
This species of false vampire bat lives throughout the savannahs and woodlands of central Africa. It is a monogamous species and can be seen engaging in courtship rituals where the male and female circle one another. Once paired, each takes turns throughout the day to protect the roost and keep a lookout for any potential dangers.

Cats

Cats originated around 25 million years ago in Asia. Whilst modern cats can be found in rainforests and mountainous terrains, many of the best-known big cats, such as lions and cheetahs, live in open grasslands. They are carnivores with athletic bodies, and are famous for their stealth and speed: the fastest creature on land is the cheetah, which can reach speeds of up to 104 kilometres per hour.

Cats have good eyesight, even in dim light, their ears and sense of smell are sensitive, and their whiskers pick up sensory information to help them hunt at dusk. In order to stay hidden, many cats have coats that are camouflaged with spots or stripes to blend into the light and shadows of their surroundings.

When stalking prey, cats crouch low and move forward slowly until the last moment, when in a flash of speed they run down their victim and snatch it with their strong claws and sharp teeth.

Domestic cats are descended from wild cats, appearing relatively recently around 10,000 years ago. They still show their hunting abilities today, catching millions of birds and small mammals every year.

─────────────── *Key to plate* ───────────────

1: Clouded leopard
Neofelis nebulosa
Length: 89 centimetres
This rarely seen species is excellent at climbing. It is under threat due to the deforestation (at the fastest rate on Earth) of its habitat in South-East Asia.

2: Lion
Panthera leo
Legnth: 285 centimetres
Second only to the tiger in size, this big cat is immediately recognisable thanks to its mane. It lives in prides where the females hunt together for food.

Hoofed Mammals

Hoofed mammals vary wildly, from the huge and powerful rhinoceros to the elegant gazelle. Despite differences in appearance, hoofed mammals all have toes strengthened by a thick, horny covering similar to toenails, which never stops growing, and is worn down by constant use.

Many have horns or antlers made of bone protruding from their heads, which they use to defend themselves from predators. Some species, such as deer, will demonstrate their strength and superiority by locking horns with a rival, hoping to impress a female and win the right to mate with her.

Typically, hoofed mammals are grazing herbivores, eating a diet based on shoots and leaves. They have wide, flat teeth suited to grinding down vegetation, and most have multi-chambered stomachs, which extract the maximum nutrition available from this difficult-to-digest food source. Often, these animals 'chew the cud', regurgitating partly digested food into their mouths, which they chew further and swallow down again.

Some, such as wildebeests and bison, move in huge migratory herds, travelling thousands of miles every year to find new grazing pastures as the weather changes through the seasons and food sources become scarce.

───────────────── *Key to plate* ─────────────────

1: Hippopotamus
Hippopotamus amphibius
Height: 1.5 metres
The African hippopotamus, whose name derives from the ancient Greek for 'river horse', wallows in the water by day and leaves to graze at night on nearby grassy pastures. It lives in pods of up to 30 animals and is an aggressive creature, holding its own in crowded swamps with crocodiles.

2: Indian rhinoceros
Rhinoceros unicornis
Height: 1.85 metres
The Indian rhino is a smaller relative of the better-known white rhinoceros. Its single horn is smaller, and it has heavy folds of thick skin with wart-

like bumps on its behind. Although generally a solitary creature, it shows friendly behaviour towards other rhinoceroses, bobbing its head and rubbing noses in greeting.

3: Reeves's muntjac deer
Muntiacus reevesi
Height: 43 centimetres
This small and stocky deer originated in China, but now thrives in forests around Europe since being introduced in the early twentieth century. It has short antlers, which can regrow if damaged, and prominent canine teeth.

4: Gerenuk
Litocranius walleri
Height: 92 centimetres

The East African gerenuk has evolved to have long legs and an elongated neck, allowing it to eat leaves from the tops of shrubs and bushes that other species cannot reach. If threatened by a predator, it turns and flees, galloping away at a high speed.

5: Masai giraffe
Giraffa camelopardalis tippelskirchi
Height: 5.5 metres
The African Masai giraffe is the tallest land mammal on Earth. Its long legs and neck have evolved to allow it to feed from the treetops, and its long and flexible tongue extends to gather in twigs and leaves. When competing for a mate, males duel by battering one another with their long necks.

Sirenia, Pinnipedia and Cetacea

Sirenia are the order to which manatees belong, and they are the closest living relations to elephants. Pinnipeds are commonly known as seals, and are semi-aquatic carnivorous mammals, related to bears and wolves. Cetaceans, like whales and dolphins, are closely related to hoofed mammals, such as hippopotamuses. The largest creature ever to have existed on Earth – the blue whale – is in this order. All have evolved to live in water, with limbs that have adapted into flippers and a tail.

Despite spending the majority of their lives underwater, these creatures have retained their mammalian need to breathe air into their lungs. As a result, they have become excellent at holding their breath – some can last for up to 30 minutes without needing to resurface. Whales and dolphins take air in and expel carbon dioxide out through a blowhole located at the top of their heads.

Like bats, water-based mammals locate prey by using echolocation. Because water carries sound waves better than air, some creatures are able to communicate across long distances: famously, humpback whales 'sing' to one another and their low-frequency sounds; can travel up to 16,000 kilometres.

Key to plate

1: **Humpback whale**
Megaptera novaeangliae
Length: 14 metres
The humpback whale is often seen breaching the water and slapping its tail. It communicates with other whales with its loud and complex song.

2: **Amazonian manatee**
Trichechus inunguis
Length: 2.4 metres
Like elephants, this herbivorous creature has a constantly replenishing set of teeth. It spends much of its day asleep.

3: **Narwhal**
Monodon monoceros
Length: 4.5 metres
The narwhal has a long, spiralled tusk. Its specialised diet of Arctic sealife makes it especially vulnerable to the North Pole's changing climate.

4: **Short-beaked common dolphin**
Delphinus delphis
Length: 1.8 metres
This intelligent and sociable creature lives in groups of hundreds, if not thousands, of other dolphins. It is well known for its aerial acrobatics.

5: **Weddell seal**
Leptonychotes weddellii
Length: 3 metres
This relatively large and common species of seal is typically found around the South Pole. It can stay submerged for up to 80 minutes.

6: **Walrus**
Odobenus rosmarus
Length: 2.9 metres
The walrus has prominent tusks, which can grow up to one metre long. It uses these tusks to compete for a mate, and to dig holes in the ice.

Habitat: Arctic Tundra

Around the North Pole is a cold, barren area called the tundra. This habitat is one of the most difficult places to survive on Earth due to its freezing temperatures, high winds, lack of shelter and scarcity of food and water. The ground is permanently frozen (a condition known as permafrost), which makes it difficult for trees and plants to grow. This means there is little vegetation for animals to feed on.

Cold-blooded reptiles and amphibians are not at all suited to this environment, but mammals can survive because they are warm-blooded and have evolved to grow warm furry coats that keep them from freezing. The thick coat of some Arctic mammals changes colour through the seasons for camouflage, turning white for the snowy winter and a darker colour through the summer.

Staying warm in such a cold habitat uses a lot of energy, and consequently many of these mammals, such as the Arctic wolf and polar bear, are carnivorous predators, feeding on protein-rich meat.

Polar bears are perfectly adapted to living in the icy tundra around the North Pole. They are classed as aquatic mammals and are master-swimmers, able to travel up to 320 kilometres in the water. Their white coat is made up of clear, hollow hairs which keep them warm in the Arctic water and dry out quickly when they are back on land.

Key to plate

1: **Polar bear**
Ursus maritimus
Length: 215 centimetres
The solitary polar bear travels far and wide in search of food, as the Arctic ice melts in the spring and freezes in winter. It has been known to cover territories of 1,000 kilometres from north to south. To protect its paws on the ice, the soles of its feet are furred.

2: **Muskox**
Ovibos moschatus
Length: 210 centimetres
The sociable muskox lives in small groups of five or six in the summer when food is plentiful and the weather is mild. In winter, these groups form large herds of up to 60 creatures for warmth and protection.

3: **Arctic wolf**
Canis lupus arctos
Length: 109 centimetres
The Arctic wolf lives in a family pack with a defined social hierarchy; the alpha pair – who are often the parents of those lower down in the pack's hierarchy – are at the top. The pack works together to hunt and care for any young pups.

4: **Arctic hare**
Lepus arcticus
Length: 56 centimetres
The Arctic hare eats woody plants, buds and grasses, and uses its keen sense of smell to find food that is buried beneath the snow. It is fast and agile, and can escape its predators by running at speeds of up to 64 kilometres per hour.

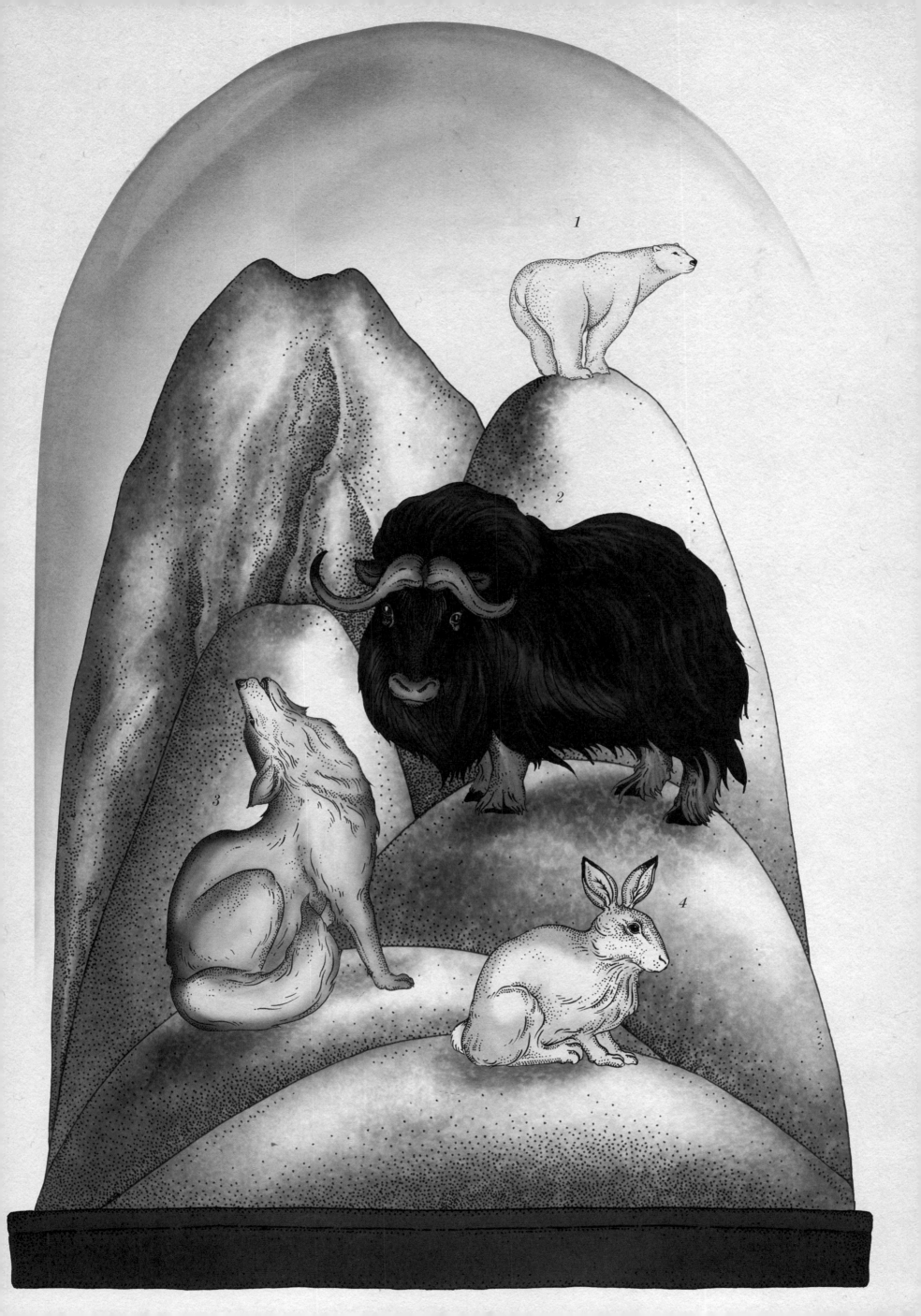

Library

Index

Curators

Katie Scott studied illustration at Brighton University and has since worked with the BBC, the *New York Times*, and Universal Records. She lives and works in London.

Jenny Broom studied at the Slade School of Art in London. She is an experienced editor and has written several books for children. She lives in London.

To Learn More

All About Birds
An online guide to birds and bird-watching by the Cornell Lab of Ornithology
allaboutbirds.org/

ARKive
A compendium of life on earth created by Wildscreen, a conservation organization based in the UK
www.arkive.org/

Monterey Bay Aquarium
Profiles of marine creatures, from anemones to zebra sharks
www.montereybayaquarium.org/

National Geographic
Animal profiles and articles about conservation efforts
www.nationalgeographic.com/